Losing me, Finding Me

Change habits, lose weight
and create a new you

Cynthia M. Spencer, MBA, MDiv.

BALBOA.
PRESS

A DIVISION OF HAY HOUSE

Balboa Press books may be ordered through booksellers or by contacting:

Balboa Press
A Division of Hay House
1663 Liberty Drive
Bloomington, IN 47403
www.balboapress.com
1 (877) 407-4847

Print information available on the last page.

ISBN: 978-1-9822-2834-7 (sc)
ISBN: 978-1-9822-2835-4 (e)

Balboa Press rev. date: 06/05/2019

GRATITUDE

I am thankful for the Spirit within that upheld me and pushed me onward in my journey to integrated wellness. It is the Self with a capital S that kept teaching and loving the self with a lower case s who had gone her own way, losing weight, gaining more.

However, we humans are not made to live alone and without the encouragement of family and friends I could not have lost 140 pounds or persevered in learning how to maintain and keep healthy. This book is about changing habits and most of the habits I changed came from suggestions and observations of others.

There are more, many more who supported and encouraged me on the way, whose names I do not know. I mention only two here, a clerk in a clothing store and a grounds maintenance man at a resort. I mention these so you will understand how very important your smallest moment of kindness may be to another. I had entered a clothing store to look at a blouse that I thought I could wear for my birthday. I decided to try it on.The clerk stepped up to the rack and found my size without asking and handed it to me as she turned to lead me to the dressing room. Tears welled up in my eyes as I saw that she had given me a size small. She recognized me as small. I used to wear 2 x! A year later and very close to goal weight, I was looking for a hiking trail at a resort. Not finding it I asked direction from a man in the grounds maintenance building. He took me to the entrance of the trail. I guessed he was concerned that I might get lost and wanted to remember what I looked like so he said "black pants, yellow top…then he stopped, looked up at my face, grinned and said. "You are gorgeous". So I am gorgeous I tell myself looking in the mirror. And I thank the man who told me so.

With your help and encouragement
I made my goal and wrote this book. Thank you.

CONTENTS

INTRODUCTION

"Health can be found only by obeying the clear cut laws of nature"
Dr Henry Bieler

You are invited to begin a three month adventure to learn about you. This is not a diet plan. It is a chance for you to look at the many decisions you can make that will help you lose your excess body weight and find a happy healthy you. You can do this by changing habits. You might call it a project. Together we will explore the many parts of integrative wellness that contribute to a healthy body.

There are laws of nature within which we live as part of our physical being here on planet earth. When we ask for, envision and expect something it is likely to come to us, unless we put out a road block. This project is about recognizing those road blocks, removing them and making new habits. An unseen spirit is there to help make our desires come to fruition. It is the magnificent Self that created you. You are the me without a capital and the Me with a capital is the perfect part of you as you are meant to be. It is what created you and me and all of us. There are many others who are available to help each of us be that healthy integrated human who lives here now. I have lost 140 pounds on my journey to wellness. I am walking with you on your journey.

Understanding the laws of nature means much work on our part to learn and act in accord with the truth we uncover about our own behavior. There are layers of perceived notions of what is true, honest and lovely, of what is excellent. Only when we work through those layers, laden with judgements and life commandments of other humans, often times built on centuries old layers, only then do we arrive at the freedom to make our own decisions that become the foundations of our integrated wellbeing.

We have the right to choose the life we want to live

This workbook is about losing those layers inside us of years of excess fat, of lists of shoulds, of big concrete blocks of I can't. It is about walking naked into a relationship with God and being clothed with Self love having experienced the depth of universal compassion, kindness and forgiveness and knowing there is more love anytime we want it. It will manifest as Love and health through us.

Some of us have spent the better part of a century weighted down by excess flesh as well as conflicting and binding self images and rules we don't want to obey because they don't make any sense to us. To reach our personal freedom may seem too daunting a task. To quote Sam, a character from "The Hobbit" who says to Frodo, who is in a state of panic about the journey ahead, "For starters, Let's just get down the hill."

Getting down the hill for us will be starting with our own bodies.

We will explore ways we can lose pounds through changing habits. If you are diligent you will have made good progress in three months in discovering the magnificent, beautiful person you were designed to be.

We are working with:

Nutrition Fitness Sleep Emotions Mind Spirit
Stress Mindfulness Visioning Relationships

to allow them all to work together under your own guidance to create a balanced integrated and happy you.

How it works!

Every week you will have a lesson for each of the 5 week days to read (1-3 pages), to understand, and follow-up with answers to questions or actions. It is suggested that you have a journal in which to write the answers to questions and make notes as you go, but you can also write in the spaces provided in the workbook.

You have the week-end off for time to catch up if you missed a day. There will be a week-end page with reminders, encouragement and an affirmation. You will be asked each week to note habits you want to lose or add. If you are meeting with a group weekly you can weigh in then, if you like or not.

This project is meant to inspire, inform and encourage you. So there is nothing included to cause a response of "guilt". The only "rules" you break are yours. I suggest walking daily, starting at 5 mins a day in the 1st week, ending at 60 mins a day by the end of 3 months. You are the one who decides how healthy you will be and how fast.

You can do this class by yourself but in most cases, it works better to meet in small groups weekly for about 1 to 1.5 hrs. I hope you have as much fun doing this, as I did in writing it and living it. My favorite celebration at the end was buying size small and x small clothes, having started at 250 pounds, wearing size 22 (2X). Not all the weight was lost in three months, but over years. Three months is a good start

"For Starters, let's just get down the hill."
Sam to Frodo

Lesson 1: Stepping into a new life

"Whatever you can do or dream, you can begin it.
Boldness has genius, power and magic in it. Begin it now"
Goethe

Those of us overweight usually get just enough help to pacify our current distress. The doctor may say your health is in danger after some breakdown (knees, heart, intestines, immune system etc.) then they abandon any further support saying come back and we'll get blood work done. We live in a brave new world in the 21st century and there are doctors who work to integrate our entire life style and will coach us and provide education to help us. I am privileged to have one of those doctors.

Without support and education we often lapse back to the same weight and many times even gain more. We lose commitment and the courage to change life habits. We are sincere in wanting to change but solution oriented participation (go on the "whatever diet", join the gym) isn't enough to get through our life commandments that are preventing our change of mind. The mind has to change because that is what is driving our behavior. That is what attracts the "I can't", 'It won't work", "That's the way it always is with me, my family etc." The commitment is shallow because deep down the beliefs are not congruent with what we say we want. WE don't believe it can happen.

We often blame our family of origin for genetics or "this is the way we lived". We blame the painful experiences we have had of loss, lack of acceptance, unkind behavior of those in authority over us. Mostly we blame ourselves for not being good enough, strong enough or courageous enough. Accepting ourselves as whole and beautiful and healthy is the beginning of any major change in our lives. Loosing extra weight that we have carried around for years is a wonderful beginning. You are embarking on what may be the deepest, most enduring and most rewarding work of your whole life.

Be brave and begin this profound journey of inward/outward transformation. My life has made a radical change as I experienced taking off over 100 pounds. In the silence of my finally "being still" I could envision the healthy me, free from destructive habits and all kinds of help began to appear for me.

This first week together I encourage you to make the commitment to begin. Some years ago a friend named Alan, sent me this quote from Goethe(1769-1832) a German writer. I offer it to you as one of many references from courageous people who offer us support and encouragement along life's way.

Goethe's Challenge to Begin

"Until one is committed, there is hesitancy,
the chance to draw back, always ineffectiveness,
concerning all acts of initiative (and creation).
There is one elementary truth, the ignorance
of which kills countless ideas and splendid plans:

That the moment one definitely commits oneself,
then providence moves too.
All sorts of things occur to help one that would
never otherwise have occurred. A whole stream
of events issues from the decision, raising in
one's favour all manner of unforeseen incidents
and meetings and material assistance which no one
could have dreamed would have come his way.

"Whatever you can do or dream, you can begin it.
Boldness has genius, power and magic in it.
Begin it now"

Questions/assignments for you:

1. Why didn't other programs to get rid of extra weight and keep if off, work for you?

2. Please write a short paragraph about why you are committed to this 12 week class? Why is it important to you?

3. Please weigh in and take measurements today.
   Weight _____ waist _____ bust/chest_____ thighs_____

"Less is more"

WEEK 1

Lesson 2: Get moving

As a single footstep will not make a path on earth,
so a single thought will not make a pathway in the mind.
Henry David Thoreau

During the course of our 12 weeks together we will focus on ways you can "get moving" each morning. They are stretching, walking, qigong and yoga. There are several days we discuss sleep, today I only want to mention those moments when we awaken and begin our day.

Have you ever noticed how cats and dogs behave after lying in sleep for a while? They get up and stretch. In Yoga we have what we call the "Dog pose". That is their early morning stretch. Try every morning to stretch your arms and legs while you are still in bed and second time just after you "hit the floor". See that's not so hard. Little steps to begin a routine of morning stretch.

You are starting this class because you are overweight, so it may not be easy. Just do as much stretching as you can without pain. Try what you can. It will help you be proud of yourself in 12 weeks when you can do better.

The only 12 week practice you are asked to do is **daily walking.**

As we begin, I am asking you to commit to a daily practice of walking. I suggest at the end of the 12 weeks that we are all walking for 60 minutes. In most cases of easy walking an hour is 2 miles or more. This is a practice to keep you healthy. It is easier than qigong or yoga or even stretches, which we will introduce other days. You can do all four of them, as I do or just one or something else that serves the same purpose. If you already walk a good amount daily, then choose some other practice to do daily in increasing amounts. Maybe you walk but know that you also want to be stretching or do yoga poses or qigong movement or just be still and have had trouble sitting quietly in meditation. Substitute what you wish and follow the same pattern for 12 weeks.

Here is the walking program, very simple

Start week 1 walking for 5 minutes daily.
each subsequent week add another 5 mins,
So week two you are walking 10 mins,
Week three 15 mins, week four 20 minutes, etc
Until at week 12 you are walking 60 minutes.

This may seem ridiculous at first. You will walk 2.5 minutes and turn around. There are some people who are following this course who do not walk at all or are overweight enough so it is hard. If you need a wheel chair, a walker or cane use the walker or cane or increase your strength by trying to move your wheel chair by yourself.

Most days, I do not walk 60 minutes at one time, but 30 minutes in the AM and 30 minutes in the PM. Doing this, in the long run, has given me the endurance to go hiking with friends for 1-2 or even 3 hours. So when you get to 30 minutes you may want to go to 15 mins am and 15 mins pm. That is still only 7.5 minutes from start until you head back.

If you are not able to walk outside, walk inside. It helps to put some music on and walk to a tune. Or you could use ear phones and walk to a cd lesson. My friend Carol recommends a Fitbit. It is worn like a watch and tracks your steps.

If you are in a wheel chair you could try moving the chair with your arms for longer than you usually do or choosing some other practice, or ask a friend to take you out for a stroll in your chair on a regular basis. If you are in a wheel chair and overweight, this 12 week adventure is especially important for you. Your life will change drastically if you are not overweight!

Whatever your reason for "I can't"... please make every effort to push through to a solution for a way you can find to "get moving" that is safe for you. This is an adventure that is much more important that traveling into outer space. "Begin it now".

Walk 5 minutes every day. Keep track here:
M___ T___ W___ TH____F____SA____SU____

Ok, you can't get very far in 5 minutes, but doing it daily will make the next week easier. Remember you are forming a habit. This is the only thing you will do as "home-work" all 7 days. That includes week-ends. You are free on week-ends from reading or answering questions. I will just include inspiring quotes on those days.

If you were unable to read one of the days, use week-end time to look at the daily lesson you missed. By the way, the questions are only for you, no one will check them.

Have fun walking

Lesson 3: Sleep for stamina

The truth is life would be easier for our bodies, minds and emotions
and everyone else we encounter during the day
if we got enough sleep!

Right here at the beginning, we introduce "sleep". Your food is digested and your body replenished with energy, many little cells are making repairs and getting you ready for another day, all during sleep. When you do not allow your body to replenish during sleep, you look for food for energy. Oh maybe you don't do those midnight snacks! like the rest of us.

The truth is most people do not get either enough sleep or a good quality of sleep. What happens when you don't get enough sleep? We all know some answers to that question, which might be falling asleep at the wheel and increasing the possibility of an automobile accident, loosing your temper with a client, possibly loosing their business, offending a mate, family member or friend and leaving a minus balance in the "love" bank, or you name it.

What is also important is that insufficient sleep can seriously impact your body's systems, and can affect the quality and possibly the duration of your Life? We will come back again several times in this course to talk of sleep.

Professor Craig Heller of Stanford University says "long term sleep deprivation can cause your physiological systems to be seriously affected and have long lasting effects." My study with him was my wake up call! Do you get enough sleep? I didn't. I burned the candle on each end for years. My greedy little mind wanted more, more information, more knowledge and understanding. I would read a book, find something I didn't know about and and stop to google more info and wind up with lights out at 1a.m.,2, 3, even a couple of times at 4 or 5. I was also writing poems, thinking. I was alive and excited and having passed the circadian cycle, I snacked and had more coffee and still got up at 6 or 7 am, at the latest. That's 3 to 6 hours sleep on the average, not enough! I stayed overweight, eating to keep me functioning in the wee hours of the night.

Why we need a good night's sleep:

Lack of sleep has caused major disasters, like multiple highway fiascos, oil spills, airplane crashes. It is as necessary to a healthy life as nutrition and exercise. Most of us are not involved in major disasters, but we have experienced a lower level of performance on the job, doing athletics or just keeping our home clean and safe, when we have not slept well. Lack of sleep also affects any psychological or psychiatric issues and contributes to many other illnesses.

Are you still going over the stuff you read on your computer last night? Do you wake up groggy? wanting to stay in bed? afraid to meet the day? If you do, there is a good chance the cells in your body are screaming at you to give them some real rest! My uncle used to say we should wake up with alacrity and zeal. First time I heard that, I said "Who are they?" Then whenever he'd say it, I'd say "who are they?" and laugh. Sometimes when I wake up and want to go back to get more sleep, I smile and say to myself "Hey, Alacrity and Zeal are you there? Come get me up." But the truth is life would be easier for our bodies, minds and emotions and everyone else we encounter during the day if we got enough sleep.

Nutrition, exercise and sleep are the three major contributors to a healthy body. I begin with sleep because of the three its misuse can cause more deadly consequences faster than can nutrition or exercise. Consequences of poor exercise can take years to develop and a person can go for days without food and much longer with minimal food. Inadequate sleep can cause us to quickly make poor judgements with friends, at work, driving and most importantly in our thinking. Sometimes when I haven't had enough sleep or when I am with someone who, it appears, may not have slept well, I think "Bad hair day!" Not that it has anything to do with hair, it is really that our body, mind and emotions are out of sorts due to lack of adequate sleep.

Questions:

How much sleep are you getting every night now? average from _____ to _____.

How much sleep to you think you want to have every day? _____

Which of the above effects of sleep debt do you have now going on in your body?

_____

_____

_____

Practices:

Please note every day this week how much sleep you had the night before.
Last night I slept _____ hours…just for this week.
Day 1
Day 2
Day 3
Day 4
Day 5
Day 6
Day 7

References

Many of the comments throughout this class about sleep come from my own experience, from tales told to me and from 2 classes (24 sessions each) see below.

Professor H. Craig Heller, **Secrets of Sleep Science: from Dreams to Disorders** Sanford University, (The Teaching Company 2013) Information from Dr. Heller's class is backed by recent research on sleep.

Professor Jason M Satterfield, University of California,S.F., The Teaching Company 2015. **"Cognitive Behavioral Therapy: Techniques for retaining your brain,** Lecture 18: Getting a Good Night's Sleep.

Lesson 4: Assessing your fitness

During week 1, and even into week two, we are doing assessments. Where is your starting point? Actually setting your weight goal comes in Lesson 7 next week. There is a long journey to the end of 12 weeks to a healthier you and it can seem overwhelming.

Sometimes we just have to trust the natural processes of the Universe which I believe are always here guiding us. It is not for us to know all the answers, sometimes just to know we must move forward and the way will open for us. You may not have all the answers to the questions I give you today. Most of us don't. You'll get some help here to figure out your health status and suggestions of where to go for help with the other answers.

What is your BMI? _____

I do not think that most physicians tell you what your BMI is, but if you go to a gym and sign up with a trainer they will figure it out. But you can too. BMI (Body Mass Index) is used "to classify weight status and associated health risks. The greater your BMI the greater your risk for many diseases including high blood pressure, diabetes, cardiovascular disease and cancer. In addition, the higher the BMI the greater your overall risk of death." (Mayo Clinic)

How do I know what my BMI is? You just need to know your height and weight.

1. Multiply your height in inches by your height in inches = _____
2. Divide your weight in pounds by the result of the first step _____
3. Multiply that answer by 703 _____

Say you are 61 inches tall and you weigh. 100 lbs
61" x 61" = 3721 100 Divided by 3721 = 0.02956 x 703 = BMI of 20.78

Or

you are 68 "tall weigh. 270 lbs

68 x 68 = 4624 270 divided by 4824 = 0.0559. x 703 = BMI of 39.34

A BMI over 30 is listed as obese.

How tall are you? (not 20 years ago… really today) Measure _____

How long can you walk? _____

What kind of places can you walk? _____

Or can't walk _____

What is your muscular strength and endurance? How many push ups? And squats can you do? _____

How is your heart? Your heart rate? A normal resting heart rate is 60-100 beats per min. Treadmills at fitness centers can tell you as you walk what your heat rate is. It increases as you walk more and harder.

What is your blood pressure? Normal is about 120/80. _____

The top number 120 is systolic pressure, when the heart beats and is pumping blood. The bottom number 80 is diastolic pressure, when the heart is at rest between beats.

How is your balance?
How many seconds can you stand on one foot eyes open? _____
How many seconds on one foot eyes closed? _____
Mayo Clinic uses best of three tries. The stated times for men and women with eyes open and closed according to age. Results are: younger men can hold longer than women, rates are eyes open from 44 seconds to 30 seconds. Eyes closed from 17 seconds to 3.6 seconds! Try it at home!

When was the last time you saw a primary care physician? _____

Last time you had blood work taken? _____

What was your cholesterol reading?_____ **How was your glucose Level?**_____

What do you do now for fitness? Not what you want to do, what do you do?

_____

_____

What would you really like to do for fitness? A sport, hiking, competitive sport, dancing, sailing, swimming, gym in your home etc. Imagine healthy you keeping healthy:

_____

_____

_____

Happiness Walk

Prevention Magazine once published a short article called "Take a Happiness Walk". You can instantly recharge your energy by increasing your circulation. Take your five minute (10 minutes next week) walk including these three things.You will find that you can do them walking down the hall, at work, during a break, after work, as you rise in the am...walk around the house, inside or out or around the block.

1. <u>Focus on your feet.</u> Feel the firm ground beneath you as each foot rolls from heel to toe. Try to hold awareness of your steps for 2 or three minutes.

2. <u>Turn your attention to breathing.</u> Lift your torso to stand upright and increase lung space. As you inhale, be aware that you are drawing in renewed energy. Exhale tiredness and pain. Let fresh life flow into your lungs and cells. Incidentally, this is what is also taught in Yoga, Qigong/Tai Chi and Taoist meditation.

3. <u>Mentally talk to yourself.</u> Thinking "Fresh air in, stale air out" as you breathe can help you maintain focus. Doing this allows space when your mind is not rushing back and forth thinking it needs to plan the next thing you "must" do. Just take in that fresh air.

Today or tomorrow take a Happiness Walk and note in your journal or in your workbook how you felt afterwards. If it works for you, do it on day 5 and the 2 week-end days as well, maybe it will get to be a new habit?

Walking check in

Important! The first day of the program we started with 5 mins a day walking. Check in. How are you doing? If you missed, you might want to set a specific time every day where you can walk wherever you are…even if it is at home walking around the house.

We cannot simply be interested in the possibility
of shifting our present reality and ushering in tangible changes.
We must become invested in these changes
through deliberate congruent action and mental focus.
David Alut

Reference

Mayo Clinic. *"Guide to Healthy Living"*

WEEK 1

Lesson 5: Your favorite foods / eating right

If you don't eat you lose

Dr Andrew Weil wrote *'Natural Health Natural Medicine"* to help readers take greater charge of their health. For that same reason this workbook is in your hands. Your health, your joy, your dreams, your life is in your hands, in no other.

This is your first week on an adventure that will change you, your size, your health and much more, to the degree that you are willing to change habits. During this course, you will be recognizing habits you have, learning and deciding which habits to retain, which to let loose and what new ones you'd like to include in your life.

Today we turn a light on some of our eating habits which include: purchasing food, what food you have in your home and how you eat. Each week there will be information, and suggested ways to personalize that information. There will be opportunities to observe what and how you eat, as well as, how you are helping your body attain and maintain health...or not. As we move on we will spend time on all the food categories. Today I ask you to notice what you eat most, as well as what are your favorite foods.

Calories: This is not a "diet" to count calories. However, you should know really what you are eating in a day. You can look up calories on line or I suggest that you invest in a small paperback book. I have the 2002 CTN Calories counter by Corinne T. Netzer. Amazon has the 2011 edition, used for $1.54! I hope you will look up the calories of your favorite foods and the foods you eat most.

Based on USDA guidelines, inactive women need about 1,600 to **2,000 calories per day** for healthy weight management. To estimate a sedentary woman's individualized calorie needs, multiply her body weight by 13. This equals about **1,560 c**alories per day for a 120-pound, inactive woman. If you are a senior you can take some of the calories off. This is a count for maintaining. We are not maintaining...so it needs to be less

Sedentary men ages 19 to 30 need 2,400 to **2,600 calories**; 31 to 50-year-old men require 2,200 to **2,400 calories**; and sedentary men over the age of 50 need 2,000 to **2,200 calories** each day to maintain a **healthy** body weight.

Averages from authoritynutrition.com state to loose weight an average height woman needs to eat 1500 calories per day to lose one pound and a man 2000 per day to loose one pound. You can eat a healthy diet for a lot less calories than that, so it will benefit you greatly to know how many calories, on the average you are eating. Keep count this week and you will know and won't have to count calories again.

There are many other factors that lead to weight loss and we will discuss them all during our three months together. But the "keep it simple" fact is always...**if you don't eat you lose.** Our goal is to change habits, not see how quickly we can take it all off. So just breathe, learn the calories of foods you currently love and take note of habits you might want to change.

My very favorite Foods are: List at least 5 up to 10

Food calories how often I eat this food

1.	6.
2.	7.
3.	8.
4.	9.
5.	10

The foods I eat the most are: (Add calories in parentheses after each food.)
for breakfast:
for lunch:
for dinner:
for snacks

Some dubious foods I have been eating:

What are some foods you regularly eat that you think "might" not be very healthy for you. Just note them here. As we continue you may see that they are actually healthy for you or you may want to turn them in for something that fits your new life style better.

1.
2.
3.
4.
5.

Foods I do not like:

1.
2.
3.
4.
5.

Note where you eat most of your meals this week:_____

Pay attention and make notes a few times this week about how fast/slow you eat.

_____

Make a menu for next week. **Weekly Menu Planner** is included. Make a list for the grocery store and stick to it.

Menus for week of _____ to _____

Day	Breakfast	Lunch	Dinner	snacks	water
MONDAY					
TUESDAY					
WEDNESDAY					
THURSDAY					
FRIDAY					
SATURDAY					
SUNDAY					
NOTES					

Have a good week-end

Week-end of week 1

Did you know

"Without regular exercise, adults can lose 10 percent of their muscle mass per decade of life, causing them to become weaker as they age, McCall says. Strength training combats that decline so you can move around more efficiently, lift everyday items (like heavy grocery bags or a grandchild), and look toned rather than scrawny. You can use your own body's weight, dumbbells, resistance bands, gym machines, or other equipment."

This is from SilverSneakers

On Changing Habits:

Old habits I am discarding

1.
2.
3.

New habits I am taking on:

1.
2.
3.

Comments about habits I have been working on:

Practices:

5 mins a day of walking
go on a happiness walk
make a menu for next week

Lesson 6: On Building a Balanced llfe

It might be that you have spent a long time, for some, nearly a life time, living with self care habits or lack of them, that are not only non-productive, but damaging to your emotional, spiritual and physical health, as well as to your relationships with yourself and others.

We are majoring in weight control which is part of body but none of our existence on this earth is disconnected to other parts of who we are as humans. Because of that we are addressing many other parts of us especially as they connect to the size and shape of our bodies.

In 1992 on an 8 day silent retreat I had a vision of a circular form that was vibrant pulsating yellow in the center. From the center extended 8 branches, like tree branches. All carried some of the pulsating yellow material into the branch. Some of the branches showed a narrowing of the yellow material but the branch itself widened. The color of the branches varied from yellow to orange and finally to brown.

I sat pondering this image and what came to me then has motivated my thought and actions for all these years. I began to understand the pulsating yellow as the primal stuff of life, the creative force, elan vital. It was the pure, good life-giving Source or God, which is creator and created. The orange was the pure getting muddy. The brown was like the dying or dead branches of a tree that no longer show life.

These eight branches extending out from the center showed, by color, their state of health of each of eight different aspects of a person. I understood the 8 aspects to be Emotions, Body, Mind, Spirit, Relationships, Finance (or Abundance), Re-Creation, Contribution. I understood from this image the message that if all of these areas are glowing pulsating yellow, we are living in balance and healthy.

I have taught an 8 session class called "Building a Balanced Life" which encourages people to take an inventory of these parts their life. I now work to write, teach and lead retreats under the name of a nascent business called "Walk in Beauty" dedicated to producing educational materials to address integrated, balanced living.

Emotions initiate action. Emotions provide us with joy, bliss and beautiful feelings. They can also produce confusion and lead us astray. We come face to face with emotions many times in this class.

Body is what we have to live in and it expresses our emotions, our thoughts and our Spirit. Body is how we show the world what is important. A great deal of this is about Body.

Mind has so much power to talk to the cells in our bodies, to help our emotions and think with the wisdom of Spirit. Mind is the Intelligence that allows us to create. How precious are our minds.

Spirit is us, continuing on after our bodies dissolve. It waits for our emotions to calm and our body to wait and our mind to stop talking, so we can hear the wisdom of eternity. Then we can act as part of Universal Wisdom. During these weeks we address spirit, mostly our awareness of it.

Relationships help us to learn what is important. How we are disposed spiritually and what our judging minds do and how our emotions behave themselves has everything to do with relationships, which has very much to do with our bodies. You can see that separating any of these is, in a sense, quite futile. Do the primary relationships in your life support the highest vision for yourself?

Finance or abundance is part of our world view. Our attitudes about what we have and can have connect to all the other "branches".

Re-creation is about re-building our selves. It is easiest to understand in terms of changing life views as we age. We recreate "what we want to do when we grow up" every 10 years or so. I wanted to be the mother of 6 kids and at 75 would love to have grandchildren but children to raise? not any more. Re-creation is also about changing our values, what is important to us. It is about clearing out the old that has become like brown dying trees to allow pulsing yellow life to course through us. We are all about that in this class.

Contribution is something that comes from our gratitude. You have been given, so you want to give back. A book you read inspired you, so you buy 10 of them as gifts for your friends. You grew up with little education but managed to acquire several degrees and a good job. You are grateful and donate money to help others learn how to reach their potential. You lose over 100 lbs and can now fit in airplane seats and get out of the bath tub. Some man looks at you and says "You're gorgeous"! And you want to help others lose weight.

Be patient.
Walk slowly with persistence and with the knowledge
that you have everything in you that is required
to meet your goals and have a healthy body.

Can you stand on this truth?

WEEK 2

lesson 7: Obesity and goal weights

We are beautiful and amazing creatures.

About obesity

Dr Henry Bieler in 1965 writes "the public has been warned over and over again that obesity is the nation's most serious health problem yet physicians still find it one of the most difficult of all diseases to treat…..a cycle of overeating, gaining ten pounds, going on a crash diet and taking it off, then stepping right back on the merry-go-round again is even more hazardous than remaining overweight. There is evidence now that this seesawing may be one of the causes of high blood pressure, doing damage to the blood vessels."

Fifty years later **Wikipedia** states "Obesity is a leading preventable cause of death worldwide, with increasing rates in adults and children. In 2015, 600 million adults (12%) and 100 million children were obese in 195 countries. Obesity is more common in women than men. Authorities view it as one of the most serious public health problems of the 21st century. Obesity is stigmatized in much of the modern world (particularly in the Western world), though it was seen as a symbol of wealth and fertility at other times in history and still is in some parts of the world. In 2013, the The American Medical Association classified obesity as a disease.

We can raise the level of consciousness about our own power to live healthy, whole lives by being the proven examples as we touch, awaken and support each other. Yes we can. We can reboot, reform ourselves, our habits and knowledge, as we reach our health goals. We are beautiful and amazing creatures.

Starting our countdown with some measurements:

Please document your size now so you can come back to see your progress. No one is asking you to tell them, it's just for you.

Height: If you are over 60 or 70 you might be surprised at your height. Many of us shrink! My mother was 5'3" always taller than I. By the time she was 81 she was 4'7" a loss of 8 inches. Similarly my older brother was 5'8" and at 84 is 5'1, a loss of 7 inches. At this writing I am 75, have been 5'1" since age 12 and would like to stay there.

Here are some things I am doing to prevent my shrinking. I stretch every day. I walk down the aisles of the grocery store like Mary Poppins about to burst out into song with head high and arms extended pushing my cart. Of course, I don't sing, I just smile and people smile back! If you look you will notice people in stores pushing carts bent over, way over. If you are short or already decreasing in height, then think how good tall people will feel that day when they remember someone who asked if they would please reach that box on the top shelf. You will have allowed another person to help you. And we are all the better for it when we help each other. When I am on my twice daily one mile walks, I walk with head up and shoulders back and pull my stomach in and breathe. And I feel taller. Ok,I have to fess up to this. When you visit a doctor and they measure you, stand with your head straight forward, then bend it down slightly just as they are measuring. I thought I was being so clever to stand tall and look them straight in the eyes. The truth is when you bend your head forward the top of your head goes higher than if it is straight forward. It took several doctor visits when I was told that I was now only 5 feet tall before I figured this out. Just saying.

Date: _____ **Today's weight** _____ **height**_____ **waist**_____
Upper leg _____ **Upper arm**_____

Factors regarding rates of loss:

It can be so frustrating when you are daily or weekly loosing or not loosing weight. Weight watchers suggests that you to only weigh in weekly. Frankly I don't care when you weigh in. I weigh myself every morning. Sometimes I have gone up and sometimes stayed the same, sometimes lost 1/2 a pound, once in a while a pound or 1.5 pounds.

Weigh in as you like. If you get emotionally out of sorts with the ups and downs then just weigh in once a week. We set goals in our lives and some days we are rushing to a touch down and other times it seems we are doing two steps back. The truth is we have an intention. We have a commitment. We are determined and will reach our goal. Some of the things that make a difference in the amount of daily/weekly loss are:

- How long you have been fasting? Did you eat after 7 pm?
- What you ate later or during the day
- How many calories you ate
- How fast the food is moving through your bowel or not moving
- Your emotional state; nerves before a trip or a test, or in-laws coming for dinner
- The amount of physical movement of your body
- If your body is busy fixing you because you are sick and doesn't have time to work on the fat cells
- If you are sick
- How much you slept
- And whatever else you know to be true for your body……

So the end piece is; don't take the daily weight so seriously, just keep moving, sleeping and eating small amounts of foods that are good for you. Keep changing your habits.

What is your goal?

To help you set a reasonable goal, here are well researched ranges given below by both Weight Watchers and The Mayo Clinic. I have gone 3 times to Weight Watchers and lost every time. But at 140 pounds overweight, I had a lot to lose. There is no reason why you can't do this workbook and Weight Watchers at the same time. Look up Weight Watchers online they are in almost every city. The Mayo Clinic has a Healthy Living program and has published a booklet called.

"Guide to Healthy Living". It costs about $12 and can be found in many bookstores or by email at SpecialSalesMayoBooks@mayo.edu or 800-430-9699.

Healthy Weight Ranges

Weight Watchers uses a list of Healthy weight ranges to help people decide what their goal weight will be. They state that they are used to determine eligibility for joining. If your goal is outside this range, that's fine. With that said, I give a nod to Weight Watchers. It's a great list and as long as you don't get stuck on numbers, I believe it can help us understand the weight at which we are likely to be most healthy. My own experience tells me that tall women with large bones just can't conceive of weighing 106 pounds. But that's the minimum they recommend for people of my height. I have weighed that as an adult and I felt wonderful. I could stand up straight and look down and see my toes, something I couldn't do at 250 pounds!

Height	Min (BMI=20)	Max (BMI=25)	Height	Min	Maximum
4"9"	92	116	5' 8"	132	164
4'10"	96	120	5' 9"	135	169
4"11	99	124	5'10"	139	174
5' 0"	102	128	5'11"	143	179
5' 1"	106	132	6' 0"	147	184
5' 2"	109	137	6' 1"	152	189
5' 3"	113	141	6' 2"	156	195
5' 4"	117	146	6' 3"	160	200
5' 5"	120	150	6' 4"	164	205
5' 6"	124	155	6' 5"	169	211
5' 7"	128	160			

Here is their list:

If you are taking this class with a group, a scale will be available for you to weigh in each week, if you like. For those who are taking this class alone, with the workbook, you might want to join a group because you will have the support in weighing in and being able to have others cheer you on as your weight comes down. If not, you might want to find a buddy to report to weekly. You can cheer each other on.

The best test that you are loosing weight is what you see in the mirror, how your clothes fit and how you feel walking down the street, getting in the bath tub, squeezing through tight places. I loved the first time I noticed how roomy an airplane seat felt! The mirror and your clothes don't lie. We usually lose more in our faces first. So smile at your slimmer self, as you brush your teeth and comb your hair. And keep smiling all the way to goal weight.

Mayo Clinic Chart

Mayo Clinic weights are from a 2013 study. You can see a difference with Weight Watchers, but not really much. These two listings are from about the most reliable sources you can find. Weight watchers and the Mayo Clinic are both highly respected and have helped thousands of people to live more healthy lives. In this workbook you have more information on emotions, mind and spirit than Mayo Clinic or Weight Watcher's provides. Below are excellent ideal weight assessments from the Mayo Clinic.

Height.	Min.	Max	Height.	Min.	Maximum
4'10"	91	115	5'8"	125	158
4'11"	94	119	5'9"	128	162
5'0"	97	123	5'10"	132	167
5'1"	100	127	5'11"	136	172
5'2"	104	131	6'0"	140	177
5'3"	107	135	6'1"	144	182
5'4"	110	140	6'2"	148	186
5'5"	114	144	6'3"	152	192
5'6"	118	148	6'4"	156	197
5'7"	121	153			

My goal weight is _____

My goal range of weight is from _____ to _____

Please remember that we all lose weight at different rates and there are many factors to loss of weight.

"You may wish to change your life, but your new vision remains merely talk until it enters the practice of your day".
John O'Donohue from *Anam Cara*

references

www.ncsl.org/research/health/obesity-statistics-in-the-united-states.aspx

Dr Henry Bieler. ***Food is your Best Medicine.*** Pages 142-145

Lesson 8: Beautiful me binder (visioning)

May you learn to see yourself with the same delight, pride and expectation with which God sees you in every moment.
John O'Donohue

What is the point of visioning?

The point of visioning is to create what you want to happen. Like anything you learn or create it takes work and sometimes you don't get it right. You will get there if you keep trying. You create it first in your mind. Today I am asking you to start that creation and work at it by finding pictures and words that show you the results you want. If you can't imagine it, it is unlikely to happen. So use your mind like a paint brush and allow yourself to see the healthy slimmer you.

When you do this you are actually creating an inner experience of your ideal dream of your life. Yes, dreams really do come true. Dreams do not have to originate in your sleep. Your conscious mind can create the life you want. I am not suggesting you engage in fantasy. Create a you that is possible. The truth is …the you that is really possible is, in all probability, much better than you can imagine at this point. Every time you imagine something you allow yourself to see a little further. Every time. So make your "Beautiful Me" binder and go back to add to it from time to time. I think you will find that your image of you expands. It will expand as you realize how much more you can imagine and as you see others opening doors for you and supporting you.

Write a vision of yourself at goal weight: Here are some questions to ask yourself that will help. You will have to use your imagination here. Think of yourself as the size/weight that you really want to be with habits changed and a new outlook on life! Complete sentences are not required. A word or phrase to remind you…this is just for you.

<u>What do you look like at goal weight with changed habits?</u>

<u>What kind of clothes are you wearing that are different from what you wear now? What do you want to wear?</u>

<u>How do people perceive you differently than they do now? What do they say to you or what do you want them to say to you?</u>

<u>How do you think of yourself differently at goal weight? You can't say "I am fat"! What do you say as you look in the mirror? Can you congratulate yourself?</u>

<u>What can you do in your self vision that you can't do now?</u>

<u>How does the weight loss potentially affect other parts of your health, of your life, your relationships?</u>

Start your "Beautiful Me" binder:

To do this you need:

- A binder(notebook) that is 1/2" to 1" wide with 3 rings.
- Paper, either already punched or plain copy paper that you can punch yourself if you have a hole punch.
- Glue or scotch tape.
- Magazines or ads or pencils and paints.

Directions:

- Label the spine. "Beautiful Me"
- Insert blank 3 hole paper …start with 20 pieces.
- Copy the above questions with your answers and put them in the Binder at the beginning.
- Pay attention to magazines around you and tear out pictures or words that inspire you and are a visualization of how you want your life to be as you regain your health, energy and right size.
- Paste them on the pages. It may turn out looking somewhat like a collage.
- Keep adding them as you form your vision of Healthy happy you.
- When you are all done you my want to take some of the images and make a big or small collage from the work you have collected.

Have fun!

Every stage of one's progress is made by the exercise of the imagination.
Neville Goddard

Lesson 9: A good night's sleep

We need good sleep more than ever in the history of humanity.

What is a good night's sleep?

Various people in our lives, as well as information in magazine articles and books, all cite how many hours you should sleep to be well rested. The truth is some of the answer depends on your age, your general health, the amount of "sleep debt" you are carrying and how active your body and mind are.

The amount of hours people sleep varies widely. In our electronic age I know people including the "the old me", who are up most of the night. Go for a walk late at night and you see many homes with lights on inside. I remember getting emails from people I worked with way past midnight. I know we burn the midnight oil. It is oh, too easy to do.

How much sleep do we need? The National Sleep Foundation states that children need 10-11 hours of sleep a night. Teens need 8.5 to 9.5 hours and adults need 7-9 hours." In a recent National Health Interview survey (2013) by the Centers for Disease Control and Prevention, it was reported that 30 percent of adults get less than 6 hours of sleep. I used to tell people I only needed 5 hours and could get by on 4! Another study reported that 70 percent of High School students get fewer than 8 hours per night of sleep. Both of these figures maybe grossly underestimated.

Curbing electronic input is vital to our sleep. I would not for anything go backwards in time. I feel exhilarated, grateful and expectant in both living today and what humanity can create, as we move into the future. In my life time we have been introduced to TV, mobile phones, personal computers, we can talk to people half the globe away by a few clicks on a mobile phone. We can do global business at home, press a button to start the fire in our fireplace, set a machine to record a TV program and look forward to having holographic transmission from our smart phones!

Because of this amazing range of communication devices our minds find little rest. We need good sleep more that ever in the history of humanity. Sleep helps to maintain homeostasis, that is a fairly constant internal condition of our bodies.

Personal sleep debt:

When you don't have the amount of sleep you need, you develop a "sleep debt", which like a credit card, is cumulative. Some times caffeine seems to help us get through the morning but it doesn't prevent the small sleep debts from becoming large ones. Dr Heller quotes an estimated 10,000 auto deaths every year because of falling asleep at the wheel and he thinks that is an underestimate. I go over to the side of the road for a 10 min cat nap if I get tired, but am aware that I just shouldn't be out there on the road. At the same time, while a glass or two of wine usually has little effect on driving, if you are sleep-deprived it can produce significant cognitive impairment.

Long term effects of sleep debt: Consequences of sleep loss include:

- <u>Obesity</u> and <u>weight gain</u>: some studies showed that getting less than 6 hours sleep correlated with excess body mass, whereas subjects who had 8 hours per night had the lowest body fat.
- <u>Diabetes</u>: many studies show correlation between short or disturbed sleep
- <u>Hardening of coronary arteries</u>
- <u>High blood pressure</u>
- <u>Infectious diseases</u>: lack of sleep decreases the ability to resist infectious diseases
- <u>Colds</u>: 3 times more likely to develop colds than those who get average of 8 hours sleep.
- <u>Depression</u>: "individuals with insomnia have a tenfold higher risk of developing depression"
- <u>Suicide</u>: "in one large US national survey, individuals with sleep problems were 9 times more likely to have planned suicide and 7.5 times more likely to have actually attempted suicide."

Short term effects of sleep deprivation

- <u>traffic and transportation accidents:</u> 50% of accidents involving heavy trucks are fatigue related, a study in 2007 indicated that 7 percent of all accidents and 18% of fatal accidents were fatigue related.
- <u>airline crashes:</u> mostly pilot fatigue and irregular scheduling
- <u>disaster in the workplace:</u> includes 3 well known nuclear accidents which occurred one at 2 am and two at 4 am! hours when the workers are sleepiest.
- <u>loss of production productivity:</u> costs for US have been calculated at $212 billion per year because of insufficient sleep.

Take It Slowly. You want to make permanent changes,
and these will take time to implement.
Have a good sleep tonight!

References

Professor H. Craig Heller, **Secrets of Sleep Science: from Dreams to Disorders** Sanford University, (The Teaching Company 2013) Information from Dr.Heller's class is backed by recent research on sleep.

Professor Jason M Satterfield,University of California,SF, The Teaching Company 2015. **"Cognitive Behavioral Therapy: Techniques for retaining your Brain,** Lecture 18: Getting a Good Night's Sleep.

WEEK 2

Lesson 10: Fruit

*"As a tool in weight loss the proper consumption of fruit
is unparalleled in its effectiveness and efficiency."*
Harvey and Marilyn Diamond

News alert: It is more important to know how much fruit you eat than how much protein! No.... yes.!! Here's why. Our early human ancestors "were not predominately meat eaters". Nor did they mostly eat seeds, shoots, leaves or grasses. They lived mostly on fruit. This news became available, like a bombshell, to nutritionists, dietitians and doctors through a story run in the May 15th 1979 New York Times. It explained the work of Dr Alan Walker, an eminent anthropologist at John's Hopkins University. He explained the way they have found to identify what humans were eating by studying the fossilized teeth. Dr. Walker wrote "No exceptions have been found. Every tooth examined from the 12 Million year period leading up to Homo erectus appeared to be that of a fruit eater." Fruit is what we are biologically adapted to eat.

Dr. William Mayo, founder of the Mayo Clinic stated in an address to the American College of Surgeons "Meat eating has increased 400 percent in the last 100 years. Cancer of the stomach forms nearly one third of all cancers of the human body."

Protein poisoning comes from the incomplete digestion of proteins that stay in the stomach for too long a time. Our bodies need to be cleansed of the toxic waste that accumulates in the body. Fruit is 80 to 90 percent cleansing, live-giving water. Fruit cleanses the system, but does not clog it.

"The life force inherent in fruit is unsurpassed by any other food"
Fit for Life p. 63

The act of digestion requires much energy. Ever wonder why you need a rest after a meal? Whole cultures stop and have a siesta after a big meal. Fruit requires less energy to be digested than any other food. When foods enter the stomach much energy is needed, more for some foods than others. The truth is fruit doesn't digest in the stomach. Exceptions are bananas, dates and dried fruit which stay there for about 45 to 60 minutes. In 20 to 30 minutes most fruit has passed through your stomach. It is in the intestines that they break down and release their "supercharged and life giving nutrients."

The authors of "Fit For Life" offer these comments; The energy that fruit conserves in passing through the stomach quickly, "is automatically redirected to cleanse the body of toxic waste, thereby reducing weight." THEREBY REDUCING WEIGHT!

"Correct consumption means that fruit should never be eaten with or immediately following anything. For most things you should wait about 3 hours, 4 hours after eating flesh food. It is essential that when you eat fruit, it is eaten on an empty stomach..... Fruit is the most important food to eat but if eaten on top of other foods, the other foods in combination with the fruit begin to rot, ferment and turn to acid." Pain can result, heartburn, indigestion. We run for medication which sometimes is even worse than a band-aid effect. Wait for at least 20 minutes after eating fruit before you eat something else. The fruit will have passed through the stomach.

Are you listening? This brings up something in my eating that is a hard habit to break.

I put fruit in my salad, along with various kinds of vegetables; raisins, cranberries, blueberries, pears, thin sliced apples. And I love it. My stomach and digestion doesn't.

I want to be healthy, vibrant and use my energy rightly. So, I make a commitment to those little cells of my body not to eat fruit in salads with veggies. But YES... to fruit salad!

Other helpful comments about eating fruit:

- eat fresh fruit, not processed by heat.
- fruit is delicate and cooking destroys potential value
- a whole fruit is better than juice
- juices of fresh fruits and vegetables are not habit forming and toxic as are: coffee, teas, sodas, and milk
- do not eat right before bed or right after arising in the morning!

- From wake up time to 12 noon eat nothing but fruit or fresh fruit juices..no limitations
- Listen to the cells in your body, when they want more give them fruit!

Questions/suggestions

1. Give it 10 days to eat only fruit from rising to noon, as much as you want. Then try a day with a big breakfast of eggs, meat, bread, juice and tell me(write in your journal) how you feel that day! I am betting you will not often return to a big breakfast of anything but fruit.

2. Take some time to look over the list of most common fruits in the Appendix.

3. Think about growing your own fruit trees! Find the places you can get fresh fruit near you.

References:

Selene Yeager and the editors of *"The doctor's Book of Food Remedies"* 1998 Rodale Press

Harvey and Marilyn Diamond *"Fit For Life"* 1985 Warner Books

Week end - week 2

"When our habits of comfort are unwelcoming to change, we experience a form of collapse. We are wired for change and change equals transformation.
As the seed that produces a tree, a flower a fruit, a bird, a person...we change...or not."
David Ault.

On Changing Habits:

Old habits I am discarding

1.
2.
3.

New habits I am taking on:

1.
2.
3.

Comments about habits I have been working on:

Practices:

10 mins a day of walking
Take your measurements
Choose a goal weight
Start a "Beautiful Me Binder"
Check out fruits in the Appendix

WEEK 3

Lesson 11: Meditation and health

As you identify less with the "self" that is you, and more with the "Self" that is the world of Love to which we all belong, you will begin to live with great ease and happiness in this world.

Awareness/meditation

When you first begin doing simple meditations, you may wonder what result you are supposed to have. They seem to be neither a prayer of asking, nor speaking to God nor an affirmation or some direct message from God, nor are they the only and complete way to alleviate stress. Yet they do alleviate stress.

At first it seems that all the effort you put into these exercises (like body scan, listening to sounds, noticing smells, different ways to concentrate on breath) is not producing anything concrete. See the suggestion at the end of this lesson. If you have never done this or are used to using your mind to make action plans and achieve results, you may be finding it frustrating.

Anthony de Mello, who was a Jesuit priest from India, known and respected for his work in meditation, and author of many books, wrote *"Sadhana, a way to God"*. The quotes that follow in this lesson are from this book, which for more than 20 years has been a guide and comfort to me.

*In the long journey to become,
what we know deeply from within us
is that we are already there.*

The lessons and peace that come to us from this simple beginning of meditation are very rich indeed. Meditation "is an exercise that brings fulfillment and satisfaction....it is to be made less with the head than the heart." The beginning of meditation, the practices that prepare one for deeper connection with God, are also those used to quiet our minds so that we may become aware. When we learn to become aware we naturally move into a life of mindfulness. We also help our emotions to be calm so we can be present with them.

This practice helps us bring our bodies to a balanced place so our little cells get into action eating up fat, reminding our bodies to have enough sleep, digesting our food and healing the systems that aren't quite working right.

De Mello ruminates about a young man who he had asked to do simple beginning meditation practices like the ones we will be doing. Referring to the young man he says, "he found it very frustrating to have to sit down motionless and expose himself to a blank, even though he admitted that he simply could not think or use his mind any other way during this time." Most of the time he spent dealing with the "monkeys" in his mind chattering at him. He pleaded with De Mello to give him something more satisfying, which he did not do.

De Mello tells us "He fortunately persevered in these seemingly frustrating exercises and after 6 months, he came to report to me that he was drawing immense benefit from them - far more than he had ever attained from other prayers, resolutions and inspirational words of others. What had happened? Nothing had changed in the exercises themselves but his life had changed!"

The attempt he was making day after day to expose himself to nothingness and emptiness, to attempt to just quiet his mind through concentration on this body, was bringing him a new power in his daily life. The change seemed effortless.

I have, from time to time in my life, attended Zen meditation sessions for long periods and spent a wonderful 5 day retreat with a Zen group. During the 5 days, no one spoke. We were asked to not make eye contact, if possible. Despite that, I have not often felt such a strong sense of community as I did then with the 20 people with whom I shared those 5 days of silent meditation.

"The change in oneself seems effortless. All the virtues you formerly tried to attain through the power of your will seem to come to you effortlessly now - sincerity, simplicity, kindliness, patience...Addictions (like food!) seem to drop off without the need for resolutions and effort on your part. When this happens to you, you will know that the time investment you made in these exercises is yielding rich dividends"

Please use these words as encouragement
and keep on daily meditating!

Practice:

1. **This week-end** give yourself a treat of quiet time for at least 15 minutes every morning and every evening.

2. **Next week** alternate in any order:

   • breathing through nose
   • breathing through mouth
   • listening for sounds
   • body scan…let your focus start at feet and touch on all the parts
   • of your body…asking them how they are, what are they feeling?
   • breathing with a mantra

Each of these practices will help you to be in a calm, peaceful state, to let go of the "monkeys that chatter in your mind. Do one of these for 5-15 minutes each day.

References:

Anthony de Mello, **Sadhanna, A way to God,** *Christian Exercises in Eastern Form,* Image books, Doubleday, 1974,1984,1991 from page 56-58

"Awareness" by the same author is a book of 57 reflections which are only 1 to 4 pages each and make for a wonderful series of daily meditations to read for inspiration.

Lesson 12: Cholesterol and fats

I hope during this 3 months you too will understand the difference you can make in your health.

How you deal with fats and your level of cholesterol is something you can regulate by your food and exercise and you can prevent the slow destruction of your body that results, for many people, in heart failure, strokes and death. One of the things that headed me to lower the cholesterol plaque in my body was watching many deaths occur during the time I was working as a hospice chaplain, deaths of people younger than I who were not taking care of their bodies. I wasn't either. I was 140 pounds overweight! It was a "come to truth" time for me! I hope during this 3 months you too will understand the difference you can make in your health. Cholesterol heavy foods taste good and are sold everywhere, so it takes more than a "good college try," as we used to say, to break learned eating habits. Let's learn a bit about cholesterol before we get to the list of Good vs Bad fats.

What is Cholesterol? How do we get rid of it?

The word cholesterol comes from the Greek chole(bile) and steros(solid) and latin olium(oil). Blood circulates, sometimes rushing very strongly, through arteries to reach each cell of the body. The lubrication oil that protects the arteries from harm during this rush of blood is called cholesterol.

It is yellowish white in color, fatty to the touch, manufactured in the liver and perfect to maintain the smooth transportation of the blood. When there is an uneven level of breaking down and building up the result can be too much cholesterol in the blood, a state we call hypercholestremia. It means the fat in the artery is building up creating "plaque" and slowing the blood from circulating through your body.

It is caused by overeating of fats and oils which are not in their natural states, usually due to over heating, especially with starch as in French fried potatoes and other fried foods. Yes, yams/sweet potato chips are better than white potatoes but they are still fried. Different factors can affect your cholesterol levels, such as diet, weight, lack of physical activity, gender and inherited genes.

High cholesterol, including LDL (bad cholesterol), has no symptoms. Even if you're eating right and taking a statin, your high LDL levels may still be uncontrolled. Because of this, it is important to have your blood checked at a lab and go over the result with your doctor. When undetected high cholesterol can lead to: Chest pressure, heart attack, stroke(or mini stroke, a TIA) or peripheral artery disease (PAD). Symptoms may include leg or buttocks pain during physical activity, such as walking. The pain goes away when the activity stops.

arteriosclerosis: hardening of the artery's walls. They loose their elasticity
atherosclerosis; fatty deposits in the arterial walls, which can slow or stop the blood flow.
coronary thrombosis: blood clotting in the arteries blocking flow to heart
aneurism: ruptured tumor in artery wall

Normal levels are;

Optimal	Borderline	high
Total cholesterol		
under 200	200-240	240 Plus
Direct LDL		
under100	100-160	over 160
HDL Cholesterol		
over 60	50-60	under 50
Triglycerides		
Under 150	150-200	over 200
non-HDL		
under 130	130-190	over 190

Foods to avoid are:

Please get your blood checked now near the beginning of your three months, so you can see the progress. If it is very high you may have to start with a prescribed medicine. However, there are over the counter suggestions as taking Red Yeast rice with Co-Q-10. Over the past 3 years my total Cholesterol has gone from 271 to 224 to 202.

Dr Henry Bieler author of **"Food is Your Best Medicine"** informs us that it is normal to eat fats but cooking them makes them "unfit for the manufacture of the perfect arterial lining." This means especially frying food in oil: french fries, fried fish, fried veggies. He explains that

Saturated fats:

are most often those with "fortified with synthetics" which may also have been heated. Examples are:

Dairy foods as butter, cream, ghee, regular fat milk, cheese, yes Ice Cream!

meats: as fatty cuts of beef, pork, lamb, processed meats like salami, sausages and the skin on chicken.

Lard (those wonderful tortillas!)

Unsaturated fats: usually foods high in Omega 3 and Omega 6 are natural unadulterated fats, which generally have no additives. Choose these.

They include:

meat fats, organ fats, marrow fats, brain fats, vegetable fats such as fat in beans, seeds, nuts (Almonds & walnuts especially), avocados, bananas and coconuts, Olive oil, natural nut butters, Many of these items are very caloric so eating them requires some balancing.

Fats do the most harm to bodies when they are used as cooking oil and heated with other foods, especially starches.

Examples are:

fried bread or potatoes, doughnuts, pancakes, pie crust, cakes, pastries and popcorn.

Bieler points out that diseases of the heart, which includes deterioration of the blood vessels are "the greatest killers of the human race, especially in more developed counties."

He suggests that we follow the rules of nature and our bodies will fare better. In 1965 Bieler wrote that 900 thousand Americans die of heart attacks every year". The number today (in 2017) is 610,000. This number comes from www.cdc.gov/heart disease/facts.htm and also states that heart disease takes 1 in 4 deaths and more than half of those are men. That's a fact that really does not comfort me as my grandmother died of a heart attack at age 70 in 1945!

Check your family history and your blood levels and perhaps one habit you might decide to change is that "traditional" family holiday recipe you just "have" to have. The general public knows a lot more about medicine, health and mind/body working than it did 75 years ago or even 30 years ago.

In general we eat too much of many foods that are not good for our bodies. When we break the physiological rules that regulate our hearts and other organs, they begin to break down. We eat too much. Yes, If we are overweigh the truth is: we eat too much.

Follow up:

For your learning

At home: check the labels on items in your refrigerator and cupboards for cholesterol levels.

Next time you buy food: check different brands for cholesterol levels.

Habits to change:

What foods are you willing to cut down on or omit that are high in cholesterol? Buy skim milk instead of regular, fat free Yogurt, skip the cheese unless it is a hard white cheese. Put veggies and basil pesto on your homemade pizza instead of mountains of melted cheese. Be creative.

List 5 high cholesterol foods you usually eat and are willing to omit from your diet for the rest of these 12 weeks?

1.

2.

3.

4.

5.

"I want to impress upon you that the means of investigation

we possess in ourselves, without the use of mechanical devices,

have yet begun to be employed"
Sir James Mackenzie

As you make differences in your eating, **your body will tell you** that it is better or balk when you offer harmful food for it to deal with. Listen and the cells of your body will talk to you. You are directly linked!

References:

Dr Henry Bieler, MD **"Food is your Best Medicine"** 1965 Vintage Books chapter 10 "Cholesterol and the troubled heart' pages 113-129

www.cdc.gov/heart

Dr. Maggie Greendwood, PHD **Good Fat, Bad Fat** 2002 The Berkeley Publishing Group

WEEK 3

Lesson 13: Veggies

"Fresh and cooked vegetables come to the rescue!"

"I don't like veggies!" Ever say that? Know people who do? Where did that life commandment come from? Adults don't usually suddenly turn against vegetables and do not, in any sort of reasonable world, come up with a ban on vegetables. It might lead us all to an investigation of where in our younger lives this notion began. We, of course, have the power to shove such unhelpful obstacles to our health into some black hole. If you have family, friends or acquaintances who are so inclined, just keep sharing your new gastronomical delights and let them learn from your joy. We have only to walk down the aisles of beautifully displayed vegetables in any grocery store to be amazed and pleased at the variety offered to us.

Vegetables as medicine

When we become burdened with diseases due to acid intoxication, usually from too many sweets, starches and proteins, we can turn to alkaline vegetables for neutralization. How wonderful is our body's ability to do this interior balancing act! (See lesson 30 for more about cleansing for healing)

Why do we need veggies?

"Veggies collect nourishment from the inorganic constituents of the soil. In the presence of water, the roots of the plant are able to absorb mineral elements found in the earth and circulate them to the leaves, where the energy of sunlight transforms them into organic compounds, containing nourishment and energy for us." Bieler page 202

The practice of eating raw vegetables has its following these days. Raw veggies are of great value, mainly for bulk and roughage, to keep the intestinal contents from becoming too dry and for rapid elimination of waste products. They also keep our muscles in strong working condition.

If you have an inflamed intestine, raw veggies may cause bleeding or worsen the condition...in that case, gently cook the veggies. For most of us a good balance of raw and cooked vegetables is wise.

About juicing

Try diluting your juiced vegetables with distilled water to make a healthy drink. Harvey and Marylin Diamond write in *Fit for Life* (page 154) "Fresh juices are the only beverages that can help you lose weight and feel great. Drink them on an empty stomach, not with or immediately following any other foods."

Some good suggestions for vegetables;

- best are the ones you grow in your own garden, even a small garden of pots
- buy fresh vegetables, if frozen buy them without sauce. Keep some canned vegetables for emergencies
- buy different types each week
- cook as short a time as possible, so they are still crisp(al dente)
- steam or boil or sir-fry with as little oil as possible (try a spray can of oil)
- flavor with lemon, pepper, garlic or herbs like basil or tarragon
- start your own herb garden in a big pot
- prepare raw vegetables for snacks: carrots, zucchini, cauliflower, radishes, turnips, celery, tomatoes and use hummus as a dip.
- in salads include a variety of vegetables and different kinds of lettuce
- use oil and vinegar, low fat yogurt as a base for salad dressings, make your own
- try some new veggies like: bok choy, artichoke, kale, fennel, daikon, etc.

"The vegetable kingdom contains our best medicines"
Dr Henry Bieler

Dr Henry Bieler

You will learn in lesson #30 how I became acquainted with Dr Bieler and his "cure all" of 4 vegetables. I do recommend you try to find his book. It was printed in 1965 and a reprint done in 1987 under the added Title "***Food is your Best Medicine: the Pioneering Nutrition Classic***" (at Amazon, new books at $8.00 and used books at $2.00).

In his small book of 230 pages he explains in detail, but does not use so many medical terms that you get dizzy. He describes the "lines of defense" against disease: digestion, the liver and the endocrine glands. He talks of cholesterol, kidneys, blood pressure, weight, proteins, and vegetables, milk and yeast, salt etc. He writes in a conversational mode which also helps you to understand how your body works and what we can do to keep it healthy. We are not just trying to lose pounds but lose bad health as we gain vibrant health that will take us safely to the useful end of these clay bodies. May we be good caretakers of our bodies.

Dr Bieler makes mention of the fact that many foods have been shunned by large populations because of commonly passed on misinformation and opinions about these unfamiliar foods. Don't we still do that? Seaweed? and other foods from cultures with which we are not familiar are examples.

Sometimes the misinformation is ignorance of the nutritional content and response to the body systems of familiar foods. Think of all the sugar we use to make our traditional holiday goodies. And we give them away as treasured gifts from long family traditions. Do we want to continue giving people gifts that shorten their lives and create less wellness? Do we?

I call on you to be brave and explore the many unfamiliar foods that help us thrive. We learn from Dr Bieler that "a stalk of celery or a serving of fresh salad greens has more vitamins and trace elements than a bottle of synthetic vitamin pills."

Some of Dr Beiler's suggestions are:

1. Use a vegetable-only diet 'as cure' when a person is "over proteinized" but not all the time.
2. A diet with low amounts of flesh, dairy and eggs is preferred.
3. Do not mix vegetables with fruits or other sweets at the same meal. Here it is again from Lesson 10...no fruit in my salad!
4. Only one starchy vegetable at a meal. Peas and potatoes, not good, need to make up a new recipe for Shepherd's Pie.

5. Root vegetables as carrots, parsnips, turnips, and beets do not digest well when cooked, as they have a tendency to create gas and acid fermentation. They are better raw...slice very thinly for salads.

6. Vegetables should be steamed or cooked in small amounts of water, use the left over water for a drink or in soups.

Questions/suggestions

1. How many servings of vegetables do you generally have each day? _____.

   If not 4-5 servings, please think about adding more veggies to your new habits list. See comment under "references" below from 2005 Daily guidelines for Americans. What could you eliminate that isn't so healthy for you? _____ and substitute with a new veggie or one with more nutrients _____.

2. Pick out some new veggies to try in the next 7-10 days. Next time you grocery shop, try at least one new veggie, or one you rarely eat. Look up ways to cook/eat it.

3. Can you grow your own? One? in a pot?

4. Enjoy your veggies today and thank them for all the ways they keep you healthy.

References

Henry Bieller, *"Food is Your Best Medicine"* pages 200-207

D.S. Thomson,M.D. editor *"Every Woman's Health: complete guide to Body and Mind"* 1985 Doubleday

Diamond, *Fit for Life,* Ibid pages 158-178

According to the **2005 Dietary Guidelines for Americans,** you should consume between **five** and **13 servings** of fruits and vegetables each day. This is equivalent to about 2 1/2 to 6 1/2 cups daily, depending on the amount of calories you need to consume for your weight and level of activity.

WEEK 3

lesson 14: Walking

"I like to think of walking as an art form
and of every walk as a painting-in-progress."
Maggie. Spilner

Where are you now in your daily walking?

On schedule? If so you are walking 15 minutes every day, 7.5 minutes out and 7.5 to return. And I will guess not finding it so hard. I'd like to encourage you to get serious about walking as a major permanent exercise in your life. The cost is a pair of good walking shoes and taking the time. If you are unable to get new shoes now, use the ones you have and take stock of how well they are doing after reading the rest of this lesson. Your shoes make a difference for many parts of your body. Be kind to you.

The benefits of walking are legion. Here are some of them.

Walking relieves stress, as it keeps your immune cells tuned up for action by increasing their action up to 57% which can last as long as 3 hours

It supports weight loss and weight maintenance.

It reduces the risk of heart disease and stroke.

It fends off diabetes by improving the body's ability to use insulin.

It eases the pain and stiffness of arthritis.

It keeps bones strong, which prevents osteoporosis.

In women, it relieves premenstrual and menopause discomforts.

It improves sleep.

It builds strength, flexibility and stamina.

It enhances mental function.

It counteracts anger, depression and anxiety.

One of the best books I have found to summarize, yet give you details of what walking does to keep you healthy, is "Prevention's **Complete Book of Walking**: everything you need to know to walk yourself to better health, by Maggie Spilner. It is full of studies to prove what she is saying, written by a woman who was not healthy and became so by walking.

My own endurance has increased greatly because of my daily walking. I have yet to walk the 26 mile Big Sur Marathon. It sounds like a good goal. I have walked a 3 K marathon and am working on the 5 K, and being able to run all the way. Not there yet, but I'm walking on! I started walking when I weighed 250 lbs (at 5' 1") because I had to walk my Greyhound and I had just bought a new camera to hone my photographic skills.

I love nature and taking my camera allowed me, along with stopping with the dog, to begin slowly. My dog can run at the rate of 35-45 miles per hour, or could before he retired. But he loves smelling and stopping so much that we just go slowly. As I got closer to my goal and my weight dropped, I have had much more stamina for walking longer distances.

Walking equipment:

Trekking poles

If you are off on hikes you may want a walking stick. Many walkers use a metal walking stick that has a pointed end. This helps dig in to the soil if you need to in order to steady yourself. Some use two sticks making it look like you are off on a skiing adventure. Prices ranges from

$10 up to $20 and more. They are often called trekking poles. You can find them at sporting goods stores, Walmart, Kohl's, Overstock and other places where you can purchase online with home delivery.

Walking shoes

But the most important equipment you need is a good pair of walking shoes. The prices run the gamut from $15(my favorites from Big Five sporting goods) to those that cost several hundred dollars. You will find big selections from $40-60, which you can buy online or in the store. Make sure you measure in a store the first time you purchase walking shoes and have a salesperson assist you in deciding on narrow, medium, wide, extra wide, as well as which ones fit your feet. They should last you a good six months to a year, depending how much you walk.

When you are shopping make sure the shoe fits the contours of your feet, bends with your foot and allows you plenty of room in the toe. You may be walking with heavy socks in cold weather. And if you are walking down hill your toes can cram tight in shoes that are not roomy enough. "A good shoe supports and stabilizes your ankle so it does not roll inwards". Make sure you have arch support.

About *Eva*. *Eva* is a shock-absorbing foam that is soft, light and flexible. It is found in the soles of many good walking shoes. Ask the salesperson, if it is not advertised as present in the shoe. *Eva* compresses on long walks, but springs back after a day of rest. Some shoes have dual density *Eva*, which means that the material has two different compression rates.

The advice below is quoted from **Complete book of Walking** page 48.

Time to buy new shoes

"To keep your feet, ankles, knees and lower back healthy and injury free, replace your walking shoes every 500-700 miles. (this means once a year if you are walking 2 miles every day). Beyond that distance, even if the shoes don't look worn-out, their shock absorbing capacity is no longer as good as what it used to be.

If you are not sure how long you have had your current shoes, set them on a table and examine them from the heel. Does the heel show any signs of wear? Does the upper look as though it has been pushed toward one side by your foot? Then it is definitely time to invest in a new pair.

On the day of your purchase, mark the date inside your shoes with a permanent marker, or in a log book. Then using your logbook you will be able to track your mileage, so you know when you will be needing a new pair. Or if you consistently walk say 3 miles for 5 days a week(or 15 miles a week) you can mark the expiration date of your current shoes on your calendar.

Ideally you should have two pairs of walking shoes on hand rather than just one. That way you can allow each pair to dry out completely after each use, minimizing foot odor and creating a less hospitable environment for bacteria and fungi. Plus, when you buy a new pair, you can switch between them and an old pair, one that has already formed to your feet. Your feet will appreciate your consideration"

Shop at the end of the day
when your feet are largest and wear your walking socks.

References:

Maggie Spilner. Preventions ***Complete Book of Walking***: everything you need to know to walk yourself to better health, Rodale, 1997

WEEK 3

Lesson 15: My emotional landscape

With God's eyes bigger and wiser than mine,
I begin a new vision of a new me.

What's your story? Or at least the first layer? Our stories are deep and rich and multilayered and they just are. They are not bad or good. But they are our stories not someone else's. They are the way, so far, we have unrolled our own scroll. They are mostly written by a "me" that has learned from pain to avoid things and from applause to seek things.

We have been surrounded by a consciousness of living that is built century upon century in family, in community, in nation and world areas. We have accepted it and conformed to it. This thing we might call race consciousness has a deep pull on us. It calls us to conform even where the conforming is not "honest, lovely and of good report". It encourages us to make judgements and categorize and build little boxes of opinion. Into those boxes we store images of ourselves and our belongings and those we care about. Into those boxes we throw the products we purchase, the movies we watch, the books we read and people we sit across from on the bus. We wallpaper the inside of the boxes with our emotions! The boxes are weighty and difficult to carry, nevertheless we carry them to every new place we move.

The only way we can break out of this is to open our eyes and see. I mean the real visual eyes, but I mean also the spiritual eyes and the eyes of wisdom. For these eyes we wait, as they say, "We wait upon the Lord." First we become still, then we begin to be aware of the God that has created all and lives and moves and is in us. Humanity has found really hundreds of names for this thing some of us call God and know as Universal Intelligence, The Great Spirit, Allness, Creator, Spirit, or Love. What ever word works for you is good. Humanity has always found a way to express that which is us, but bigger than us, the "me" of which I am a small individual part of the "Me", the self which is part of the Self.

Remain unmoving until your mud settles and the water is clear.
Tao de Ching chapter 15

I invite you to work on many levels during these 3 months. Please take the time, daily to be still, invite a peaceful presence to fill you. Below is an example of one way to be still. Another practice is being courageous enough to look at your own life. That's a pretty big proposal, so let's narrow it down today to connecting your weight at different times in your life with the emotional landscape of that period of time.

Please jot down the estimated average weight you were at the following ages. Add under "emotional issues" a few words to indicate what issues pushed your emotions at that time.

years	estimated average weight	Emotional issues. Why you stayed overweight
1-10		
10-20		
20-30		
30-40		
40-50		
50-60		
60-70		
70-80		
80-90		

Here we are relating weight gain to emotions. What got you fat? and why you stayed there? What was the story you were told or told yourself? Allow yourself to walk into that past reality and observe it, just watch. Go back and look at it, but see it from who you are now and come to terms understanding that is no longer where you live today.

Today you see a skinny, beautiful, energy filled person!!

You can become the person you want to be. There is a lot more to lose than pounds;

self images, judgements of others transferred to self judgement. What is right for you? Someone else's diet or life is fine for them. What I want for you is to get to the core, tame that beast, the uncontrolled emotions that push us to make decisions that seem comforting but are not good for us. Buy flowers to honor yourself, not ice cream...

Make an affirmation and print it out and put it on your mirror. like:

I am vibrant, happy and healthy at my goal weight!

Believe that you can accomplish vibrant health and there will be help everywhere you turn. There is help! You are not alone.

I hope what motivates you now is not to look like a model, or even fit in an air plane seat comfortably. I hope it is not to please your parents, spouse or children or to get a friend off your back. If your motivation can be to uncover the real you, then you will see that you were made to be perfect and you are perfect. When we discover that, we begin to take care of this perfect self, to respect it and love it. Please believe that you are loved and have the ability to love yourself and anyone who has been a part of your weight gain. You have a new life to live...a beautiful, abundant, full life to live.

Clearing out old lies about you, yours or theirs, starts by your seeing your own emotions that led you to a self image that you held in your mind. Now you have a new image. Today is a day to throw away old images. I suggest you do that in two ways

Practices:

Getting rid of old images:

- these may be the notes you wrote to put together your story. Take as many small papers as you want and write part of the old image on the papers. You might write such things as; not good enough, wearing oversized clothes, not lovable, embarrassed, ugly clothes, made fun of etc. Then take the papers outside in a fireproof pan or inside in a fireplace and tell yourself that you no longer want those images. Burn them or shred them. If they come back to your mind, invite them to leave. You don't need those images of yourself any more. 15 mins

Be Still and breathe

- Put a timer on so you don't need to look up at a clock. Find a comfortable place to sit with feet on the ground and no one around and just be still for 3 minutes. Don't think just breathe. Don't even think how you are breathing, just breathe. Don't count breaths, or hold your breath, just be aware of your breath. 3 mins

  It takes 2 minutes to unload the dishwasher, so this is a speck more!
  If you already do a meditation practice, do it for 5 to 10 minutes instead of 3.

Si se puede

Week-end of Week 3

I hold fast all that is good of my past, and release all that prevents
the development of my highest good.
Science of Mind Magazine 9/2016 page 64

On Changing Habits:

Old habits I am discarding

1.
2.
3.

New habits I am taking on:

1.
2.
3.

Comments about habits I have been working on:

Practices:

15 mins a day of walking
Meditation time on the week-end (see lesson 11)
Cutting down on high cholesterol foods
Add more veggies
Check walking shoes
Cull and discard old unwanted self images

Lesson 16: What is sleep?

Visualize your cells morning party!!!

Time to assess our sleep habits. How much sleep are you getting? Not eating or drinking several hours before bedtime? Does your body have a chance to digest and reach out to grab the extra fat just sitting there waiting to do a disappearing act for you? Try visualizing the cells in your body having a party every morning when they have had time for the body to stop working at digesting, so they can push the fat cells out!! They are sitting around just chewing the fat in the wee hours of the morning. Ha..bet you didn't know where that expression came from. I know because one of my cells told me about those early morning celebrations.

What is Sleep?

Some weeks ago we discussed what a good night's sleep is, today we move into understanding what happens in sleep. What is sleep really, except for a chance for the fat cells to be eliminated? It is a loss of consciousness that normally lasts 8-9 hours, if not broken up by text messages, a need to eliminate, someone cooking dinner or breakfast in the kitchen and banging pots and pans about or any of the other things that wake us up before we are ready. This state of unconsciousness has two substates: REM Sleep and non-REM sleep

Professor Heller from Stanford University admits that science does not really know for sure what the function of sleep is. However, most studies assume that sleep restores in our bodies something that has been depleted, or as I suggest, it allows our cells to eat up what they need and discard what they don't. Everybody seems to agree that sleep helps to regulate our bodies, to provide a constant internal condition, a homeostasis.

Studies, using EEG machines connected to people sleeping, have determined that the two basic states of rem and non rem sleep can be characterized in this way: During REM sleep rapid eye movement occurs and is called active sleep, desynchronized. This is often when vivid, active and bizarre dreams occur. Dreaming Sleep is REM sleep. My dog does this and his leg muscles move slightly like he is running...maybe being on the race track again? During REM Sleep we lose muscle tone and are essentially paralyzed. If that didn't happen, we would act out our dreams. Nightmares occur during REM sleep.

Non-REM sleep is synchronized, slow-wave or quiet sleep. We might say "sleeping like a baby". Some less than normal occurrences in Non-REM sleep are sleep walking, which can last from 5 to 60 minutes. This usually occurs in the first third of the night. And here is another non-REM event that, though not normal, has been reported. I quote from Dr Heller:

> "another parasomnia that is a particular category of sleepwalking or develops out of sleepwalking is sleep-related eating disorder. The individual gets out of bed, goes to the kitchen and eats considerable amounts of food. There is no recollection of the event in the morning".

Wish I could just say "oh gosh all those years it was a disorder!" I mean all those years of eating peanut butter and jelly sandwiches either late at night or waking up and making them. However, I remember! Are you a late night eater? Give those cells a chance to celebrate and clean up your body. Seriously! There are thousands of overweight people who eat on into the night. It's a big habit to change.

Circadian cycle

And why sometimes do we eat on into the night? Sometimes our minds are running fast and we just don't listen to the wisdom of our bodies. We know to stay up longer means we will eat more for energy. And we eat. We are made to operate in cycles. When we stay up very late or sleep very late in the morning, we can disrupt our circadian rhythms, the internal body clock that regulates when you feel alert and when you feel sleepy.

"Circadian rhythms are truly global features of life on our planet, and they play an important role in controlling when we are asleep, when we are awake, when we can be at optimal performance and when we get the most deep and restful sleep." (p36 Heller)

Most people experience different levels of sleepiness and alertness throughout the day. Sleep is regulated by two body systems: sleep/wake homeostasis and the circadian biological clock. When we have been awake for a long period of time, sleep/wake homeostasis tells us that a need for sleep is accumulating and that it is time to sleep. It also helps us maintain enough sleep throughout the night to make up for the hours of being awake. If this restorative process existed alone, it would mean that we would be most alert as our day was starting out, and that the longer we were awake, the more we would feel like sleeping. In this way, sleep/wake homeostasis creates a drive that balances sleep and wakefulness.(info from the National foundation for Sleep)

The circadian rhythm dips and rises at different times of the day, The National Foundation for Sleep tells us that adults' strongest sleep drive generally occurs between 2:00-4:00 am and in the afternoon between 1:00-3:00 pm. This is afternoon siesta time and eating a large noon meal also effects our sleep need as our body is busy digesting food.

Begin to notice in yourself, and you may see that around 10 pm you are getting sleepy and if you refuel by heading to the frig, you can keep awake until 2 am, a time when most give up, turn off the lights and head to bed. That's when peanut butter sandwiches began to dance in my head. Meanwhile, if you follow this pattern, you will find that those poor little cells in your body are not celebrating they are groaning at all the work given them before they had enough time to rest. Our minds need to work with our bodies and give them a break. If you have to prepare for work, rest assured that your mind will be working better in the morning. Set your alarm, if you need to, but let your body prepare to function at its best...save the calories and say goodbye to the stored fat.

If you can sleep late in the morning on a daily basis then eating during that last 4 hour period will probably not cause the deficiency you might otherwise experience. Having to live with nighttime work shift changes takes careful planning. Really, it all takes careful planning. When you stop to think about it, if you have raised children, you were careful to see that they got the sleep they needed. We need to be that careful with ourselves no matter what age we are. We need less sleep the older we are, but we need sleep. Then as our bodies approach death, we find ourselves requiring more sleep. It is a natural part of leaving. Many hospice patients even get 18-20 hours of sleep. But today, we are on a journey to lose weight and live healthy lives so the majority of us still need between 7-9 hours of sleep to function well.

Although there is some variation depending on whether you are a "morning person" or an "evening person," the sleepiness we experience during these circadian dips will be less intense if we have had sufficient sleep, and more intense when we are sleep deprived. The circadian rhythm also causes us to feel more alert at certain points of the day, even if we have been awake for hours.

Questions: We are now a 3rd of the way through our time together. It was suggested that you track sleep for the first month, if you have been keeping track, what have you discovered? _____

How much sleep on the average are you getting at this point? _____

What happens to your eating and general energy when you get enough sleep? or don't get enough sleep? _____.

Practice turning in and waking up at the same time: For a week, pick a time you want to turn out the lights _____ and when you want to rise_____. Then tell your body you want to wake up then. I have done this most of my life and it works. I was always awake when my Dad came to knock on my door and say "Rise and Shine". I'd say "Morning Dad" and go back to sleep and manage to be ready for school on time. The only time I've ever used an alarm clock is when I was taking an early air flight and needed to be up at 3 am and didn't want to risk the possibility of missing my plane.

Nowadays, it is too easy for me. I told my Greyhound to help me and he does a very slight whine at 5 am every morning, if I am not getting up. He also gets up from the living room and goes to his bed at 9:45! We have more mind power than we know and so do our animals.

"Every person is the dreamer of his own dreams, and within each is the Spiritual Power to choose the patterns that he wishes to experience in life."
Ernest Holmes

References:

Kiplingers' Magazine March 2017

Secrets of Sleep Science: from Dreams to Disorders(24 session class) by Professor H. Graig Heller, Sanford University, (The Teaching Company 201)

National foundation for Sleep

WEEK 4

Lesson 17: How you eat

How you eat matters!

Skipping meals   **Grazing on the go**   **Grocery shopping**
When you are hungry   **Eating too fast**   **Where you eat**

Skipping meals produces a slower metabolism and poor choices later, yet many of us skip a meal once a day. When we are really hungry we wind up eating more than we need and eating it too fast. When we eat a small amount slowly and wait 20 minutes, chances are we are no longer hungry. When people go shopping on an empty stomach, they tend to buy more and more of the items that appeal to the thought "oh those were good" that comes from somewhere in our history. We call them comfort foods, but in the long run they only offer comfort to the cat or dog that is enjoying a nap on our belly.

New York City's Montefiore Medical Center is quoted on CBS News saying that recent research regarding skipping meals and the overeating that follows, could be directly related to an increase in belly fat, which can lead to a number of health problems, including heart disease and diabetes." The truth is any amount of extra weight can, to some degree, influence those two diseases plus others including bad knees, compromise of the immune system, poor circulation, poor elimination and scores of other manifestations of disfunction. Our bodies are designed to be whole and perfect. We are the supervisors and maintenance crew that keeps us functioning well. Skipping meals can lead to "grazing on the go."

Grazing on the go: Ever stop to look in the frig and just take a bite of something, bring out the left over enchilada, or chocolate cake, just cut a few slices of cheese? Do you stop by the free food left at your place of work? Those chocolate covered almonds from Trader Joe's are really good, aren't they? Or maybe you carry snacks in the car? Oh I know they are really for the homeless person holding the sign and asking for donations and you get the chocolate/peanut butter bars with the most protein and give them out.

But this time you skipped lunch and reach in the glove compartment for a health bar at 4 pm. Dinner is at 6 and you eat a full meal. You don't really remember the health bar, because you were driving and talking on the cell phone and thinking about the last meeting of the day or picking up your kids at school. You were acting out what could turn out to be destructive mindlessness!

All said and done, at the end of the day, you forgot that you ate the chocolate/peanut butter bar. But your body didn't forget. Those little cells are in there talking. They are trying to figure out how to get through to the boss. It would help if you gave them permission to communicate with you. They were trying and you brushed them off.

So get serious and make a pact with them. Ask them to send up an alert and agree that you will pay attention. It really doesn't do any good to try to figure out what the alert will be. Your intellect is like the objective part of your intelligence... but the cells operate in a sort of subjective way … intuitively they know and you can never be sure when you will want food or what is setting the desire off. But they know. They know. And they can just like that, bring something across your path...like a very beautiful, very skinny woman walking across the street, just as you are opening the glove compartment. You think that's me! That's the image I have been creating. And quietly without any guilt or remorse or regret you bring your right hand back to the steering wheel. The skinny girl walks by. The light turns green and you look in the rear view mirror...move just a little to the right so you can see the big happy smile on your face. And you say "Thanks cells!"

They look at each other and say "She'll make it." And you will.

Grocery Shopping while hungry

As we noted, skipping meals can also lead to grocery shopping while hungry, which often leads to a shopping cart full of unhealthy foods, that at some time in our life were "comfort foods". Best solution, that also saves money, is to make your weekly menu ahead. Make a list of foods you need to purchase and only buy those foods. This is another habit you may choose to acquire.

Eating too fast: If you have trouble chewing your food the 33 chews some of us were told to do as kids, there are several options.

Take a bite and then put your utensil down or hand(if your hand was your utensil) down in your lap. If there is someone else there either say something and then take another bite or stop look at them and paraphrase what they just said. This gives you time to digest the last bite and it helps tremendously with personal relationships. It really is a gift to another person to listen and well enough to be able to repeat back to them what they said.

If there is no one else there, here are several options you could do, as you put your hand in your lap

a. Say a few words to your Food Angel, then continue eating. If there are other people around and you want to avoid the possibility of them thinking you are hallucinating, then have the conversation silently.

b. Say a few words to yourself. A lot of us think that God lives in us, so this may be about the same as option a.

c. Same as above only now you talk to an imaginary person. I did this when I was 12. My imaginary person was George and he was 5' 11" and had brown eyes. You might want to be careful about this. What happen to me was..at 17 I met a boy of same name and description and he was my first love. You have to be careful about what you imagine. Sometimes it appears.

d. The last option is to have a newspaper or magazine or book with you at the table and stop to read a line or two before you take the next bite.

The objective is to eat slowly so the food is digested and you don't eat as much. Most of us really only need to eat about 1/2 the amount of food we eat. What is important is the kind of food and quality of food we eat. When we eat matters too. We will come back to when we eat and to nutrition many times during the 3 months we are together. For today, think about eating slower and try the options I suggested.

Why you do better eating at the table

The options I described above are meant for eating at the table. If you eat while you are working or watching TV or watching a movie, you run the chance of eating your main meal the way most people eat popcorn in a movie, absentmindedly. Really eating like that is not much better than the way my dog eats. I've had to train him to "Wait" until I get the dog bowl down in the bowl holder. Then he takes less than 1 minute to eat 2 cups of food. But then we aren't Greyhounds. We don't run at 35-45 miles per hour. Some of us barely walk. We can talk about walking tomorrow.

Just pay attention to life

Lesson 18: Self Speak

"Divine self-confidence is a result of knowledge that the self is governed, protected and sustained by Spirit"
Ernest Holmes

We are at the last week of a whole month of losing dubious habits and making healthy ones. Our focus today is on emotions and thoughts, noticing the emotions that arise during our self talk. We talk to our selves all day and often say things that are not helpful or true. We are telling ourselves what we believe about ourselves. Like a boomerang, that is what comes back to us. We live what we believe. Soon others hear the thoughts that leak out of the hidden places in our mind, becoming the words that tell our family, friends, co-workers all the self deprecating beliefs we hold about ourselves.

Sometimes we don't dare say that we are magnificent, worthy, lovable, resilient and beautiful… even if we think it, because we have been trained to talk down about ourselves.

"You shouldn't toot your own horn!"
"You didn't mean to self aggrandize, did you?"
"Oh it wasn't me, it was God…or so and so …don't give me the credit."

It was God. It was Love. But it was Love in human form as you, the best of you, making a choice to do good. Don't deny it, just keep on doing it. Your actions change the world…little by little.

Who are you anyway?

I love the response a friend of mine had to those kind of remarks. "We are not garbage! We are God's kids." We are the creative manifestation in the world of the best, kindest and most compassionate form of intelligence. We are really Universal Intelligence in human form. Ok, we are not all of "God". God is everything. We are a small part. We were not formed to be androids, but to make decisions, to choose. Sometimes our emotions are not in sync with our highest thoughts. And sometimes we and all other humans make mistakes in our choices. Then we get back on the horse and go on, don't we?

There is a balance of living, the balance of thoughts and emotions that operate all the time in awareness of our existence as conscious expressions of that which is All. Most of us, in any spirituality, come to the point where we call that expression "Love". We can choose to think ill of others and of ourselves, but Love does not do that. Eternal Love, believes in, hopes for and cherishes all that it has created. That means you! Until you can accept that reality, it is difficult to love those who belittle or are unkind to you. When we choose to be around people like that, we begin to think and behave in unkind and condescending ways. Usually the first person we are unkind to is ourself. Our objective during this 3 month period is to lose that ego-driven person in us who is fearful and angry and wants revenge and isn't really nice to others because, we aren't kind and compassionate with ourselves. When we can lose that part of us, what we find left is the person who is Magnificent, because he or she is ***created to be so.***

Today, please take the time to listen to your thoughts.

What are you saying as you begin your day? What do you say to yourself when the car in back of you speeds up and crosses in front of you? What do you say silently when your frazzled, controlling boss (or family member) accuses you of something, whether or not you did it? What does your response tell you about who you are…deep at the core?

Whatever you are saying to yourself is important because it doesn't just stop with a thought. If you say nothing, but keep thinking the negative thought, then it travels inward through your mind, into your body..every cell, and begins to destroy your calm, your well-being, all that is the best of you. Mostly we call the result "stress' but it also becomes resentment, self directed anger and pulls you down into some dark murky place. If not dealt with, eventually it becomes disease, which causes millions of deaths prematurely every year. If you let the reaction out in full force it can be as forceful as physically hitting another person and even more destructive to them, to you and to any relationship you have or have had with them.

Whether you keep that emotion inside you or spew it out on another, there is the great likelihood that it motivates a stop for something to eat that you didn't need and only that injured part of you thinks it is healthy for you. The emotion that was not stopped, but has grown, transforms to become the pint of Talenti Pistachio ice cream that you picked up on the way home. We know that it has little chance to survive the night, anywhere but in your stomach. There goes the new habit and you are back blaming yourself for giving in to thinking you can't do it.

Take a deep breath, in and out and tell your cells to help you.
Your body will help you, honestly it will!

When your emotions start taking you places you do not want to go, do something else. Try some of the tools listed below.

Questions

1. Which if any of these things do you often or sometimes say to yourself about yourself a. I am not lovable. b. I can't go or do something because I look bad...too fat..clothes not nice etc! c. They won't accept me/ I don't really think I am acceptable/I won't be accepted. d. I am not good enough e. I'll make a mess of it.

Write in your journal or below about one or two of the above. Just a few sentences or phrases, using as many emotion words as you can to describe how you feel when you are saying similar things to yourself.

2. Do you often get caught up trying to make meaning out of other people's words or behavior towards you? Write the specific times this has happened in the recent past. Then allow yourself the kindness to think of them as not being aware of the impact of their words.

Tools:

Breathe: take a deep breath in and out and tell your cells to help you. Your body will help you, honestly it will!

Count: silently or out loud if you are alone. Doing this you distracts your mind and allows the emotion to collapse.

Write it out in your journal: This helps you to see your emotions and thoughts more clearly and many times you will be glad that the only person who heard them was your journal.

Visualize: Make an image in your mind of how you want the outcome, someone is yelling at you..visualize a calm, peaceful conversation. I have done this and seen the situation change immediately.

Change the situation; Just do something else immediately, move, bend down to touch your foot, anything so the emotion you are feeling can dissipate and not get stronger.

Prayer: bring the situation to prayer/meditation and leave it there, for a response to come, when it is time.

Don't pass it on as story, gossip or anything else. It just gets bigger and meaner. Let it go…let it float into the mist!

"I breathe through my compassionate heart and
remember the Divine as me, is me. I am worthy"
The Rev Dr Michelle Medrano SOM 9/6/17

"Father forgive them for they know not what they do." Luke 23: 34

WEEK 4

Lesson 19: Fasting

*"Apparently Mark Twain admitted in one of his articles
that he gained a reputation as a doctor by merely
telling his sick friends to do what he did "fast for 48 hours."*
reported by Dr Henry Beiler

So many different opinions on fasting!!! Look up the topic, ask your primary care doctor, ask your nutritionist, ask friends, but as for me, I am going by this advice written in the giant volume called ***"Prescription for Nutritional Healing"*** by Phyllis A. Balch. I use this because it makes more sense to me and because I have done these fasts and they work and have helped me loose my weight.

Why Fast? The truth is toxins build up in your body and you can help clear them out before the damage is done. Things that contribute to toxicity are pollutants in the air we breathe and chemicals in the food and water we consume. The body needs to release the toxins from your tissues. They enter your blood stream and produce a "low" or "down" cycle. You can experience a headache, diarrhea, or depression. Fasting is a safe way to help your body detoxify, to cleanse the body. It is also helpful for any illness. If you are ill, rest, eat little and do not eat foods that are hard to digest. Regular fasting gives all your organs a rest and helps reverse the aging process to give you a longer and healthier life.

What happens is toxic elements continue to be eliminated naturally but you take in less toxins so there is a reduction of total toxicity. The energy used for digestion is redirected to immune function, cell growth and eliminatory processes.

Fasting can benefit you in these ways:

- Heal you faster
- Clean our your liver, kidney and colon
- Purify your blood
- Help you loose excess weight and water
- Flush out toxins
- Clear eyes and tongue

Recommended Fasting:

3 day fast. (monthly)	To rid body of toxins
5 day fast (for healing)	To begin the process of healing and rebuilding
10 day fast (2 x a year)	This is preventative and helps your body be in a place to fight off illness

How to Fast:

Do not fast on water alone, as this will release the toxins too quickly, cause headaches and more. Make it a "live juice" fast as that will give you more and better quality vitamins, minerals and enzymes. It will help you get used to the taste of raw veggies and gives you increased vitality.

Warning: as you might expect…if you are going to fast over 3 days, all the books I have read and people I have talked to recommend that you consult with a health care professional, especially if you are pregnant or have diabetes or hypoglycemia or other chronic health problems.

Preparing for the Fast: eat only raw veggies and fruits for 2 days

During the fast:

- Drink at least 8 8-oz glasses of steam distilled water daily, plus pure juices and up to 2 cups of herbal tea a day.
- Dilute all juices with water (1 part water to 2 parts juice.
- Do not drink orange juice or tomato juice, avoid all juices with sugar or other additives.

- Best is fresh lemon juice (1 lemon in 1 cup of warm water)
- Other good drinks: Fresh apple, beet, cabbage, carrot, celery, grape and "green drinks" from leafy green veggies…..these are excellent for detoxifying.
- Raw cabbage juice is good for ulcers, cancer. Drink it as soon as prepared as it quickly looses it vitamin content.
- As a rule do not combine fruit and veggie juices, except apples are ok.

If you must eat: eat watermelon or fresh apple sauce made in a blender or food processor with skin on apples and raw not cooked…..of course leave off the sugar and cinnamon and raisins! You can continue taking meds and vitamins.

Following the fast Drink juice, water and teas with 2 days of raw veggies and raw fruits. "The desirable effects of the fast can be ruined by eating cooked foods immediately afterward. The first meals after a fast should be small as your stomach will decrease in size."

This will take planning ahead. I hope you will try it. It takes about 3 days but then you are feeling so good and the pounds are rolling off. Be brave and try safe, wise fasting.

"It took years to wear your body down and it will take time to build it back up to its peak condition."

Believe that it can be done.

In the future whenever you start to feel unwell, fast and feel better.
from *"Every Woman's Book of Health"*, DS Thompson,MD. Consulting editor

Lesson 20: How to be a Chinese Plate

How to be a Chinese Plate
A mindful response

Stress is a major contributor to over eating. We will come back several times to stress. Today I offer you the simple practice of watching. Watching comes under the category of mindfulness. If we are mindful of the present moment, then we are fully engaged in the present and do not have time to have emotional responses to life around us that trigger anxious thoughts. Those thoughts often take on a life of their own and our anxiety increases. The practice of watching, just watching without the need to judge, get defensive, comment or interfere in someone else's life, is a very calming experience.

We can also watch our own thoughts, as they wander into judgements and solutions, put them back in the right place, smile and walk on. Stress eliminated!

There is a wonderful old poem that embodies the position we can take in watching. It is called "The Duel" by Eugene Field. It is a silly fun poem and is a helpful way to see ourselves when cars are honking, people shaking their heads around us, yelling in a grocery store or across the table from us.

I make note of the Chinese plate but it is also the old Dutch clock that does a good job of watching. The Chinese plate reacts and pulls back. But then what can you do when you are a Chinese plate on a shelf? I hope you will allow this amusing poem to come to your mind when the occasion arises to be stressed about something in your life. Just take on the attitude of the Dutch Clock and the Chinese Plate…watch and let the time pass. It is not ours to solve all the little issues that circle around us daily.

Here's the poem **"The Duel".** by Eugene Field. (1850 - 1895)

The gingham dog and the calico cat
Side by side on the table sat;
"Twas half past twelve, and (what do you think!)
Nor one nor t' other had slept a wink!
> *The old Dutch clock and the Chinese plate*
> *Appeared to know as sure as fate*
There was going to be a terrible spat.

> *(I wasn't there: I simply state*
> *what was told to me by the Chinese plate!)*

The gingham dog went "bow-wow-wow!"
And the calico cat replied "mee-ow!"
The air was littered, an hour or so,
With bits of gingham and calico,
> *While the old Dutch clock in the chimney-place*
> *Up with its hands before his face,*
For it always dreaded a family row!

> *(never mind: I am only telling you*
> *What the old Dutch clock declares is true!)*

The Chinese plate looked very blue,
And wailed "Oh dear! What shall we do!"
But the gingham dog and the calico cat
Wallowed this way and tumbled that,
> *Employing every tooth and claw*
> *In the awfullest way you ever saw -*
And oh! How the gingham and calico flew!

> *(don't fancy I exaggerate -*
> *I got my news from the Chinese plate!)*

Next morning where the two had sat
They found no trace of dog or cat:

And some folks think unto this day
That burglars stole that pair away!
   But the truth about the cat and pup
   Is this: they ate each other up!
Now what do you really think of that!

   (The old Dutch clock it told me so,
   And that is how I came to know.)

When chaos enters, stop and watch.
Take note, let life flow and watch to see where it will go.
Send a thought for peace.
Be peace yourself and
your action will help to create peace around you.
Be the Chinese plate.
Watch.

Use this practice over the week-end.
Watch your own thoughts, as they wander into judgements and solutions.
Then put them back in the right place, smile and walk on. Stress eliminated!

Week-end of Week 4

Simply being interested lacks commitment;

becoming invested makes our aspirations non-negotiable.
David Alut

On Changing Habits:

Old habits I am discarding

1.
2.
3.

New habits I am taking on:

1.
2.
3.

Comments about habits I have been working on:

Practices:

20 mins a day of walking
How much sleep are you getting?
Listen to what you are saying to yourself
Can you plan a short veggie/fruit fast in the next 10 days?
Watch..just watch.

WEEK 5

Lesson 21: Relationships, the roots of self talk

Long before we knew ....
we learned how to speak of ourself

What are the roots of the creation of a self image that allowed us to stop caring about ourselves as a whole integrated, healthy person? Did we ever care? If we did, why did we stop? Or what made us become aware to begin again on the road to health? Today is a hard look at relationships.

In lesson 15 you wrote about your weight at different ages and what was going on emotionally and why you stayed overweight. There are people in our lives that have made a big impact on us, positively or negatively. Go back to **the first humans you knew**… to your parents, grandparents and siblings, aunts and uncles, cousins or those you raised you from infancy to about 10-11 years old. What do you remember about those first relationships? What did they say to to you? praise or criticism? What did your family say to you? Or how were you treated?

Please use the space here to jot down some notes.

You went to school. Do you remember things your teachers or fellow students said to you, especially about your body, how you dressed, but also praise vs criticism of any kind? By criticism I really mean something negative. Children learn how to behave and how to "fit in" and we are not usually scared for life if someone tells us we should say thank you or if they tell you not to hit people. But they say other things. What do you remember about your early school days and how that affected your self image?

Please write here.

What kept feeding the self talk that arose from all these experiences?

In another lesson we address ways to both think differently and to re-frame some of those scenes. First we have to be honest enough to remember the roots of our self talk. That helps us begin to see situations from our adult view. What did they say and how did we feel back then?

Forward moving actions happen
at the speed that I am able to release the old thought
and accept the new thought.

WEEK 5

lesson 22: Sleep rituals.

Improving sleep/getting ready to sleep

We come once again to sleep, one of the three most important parts to having healthy bodies: sleep, exercise and nutrition. We know that our beliefs, attitudes, emotions, work situations and relationships with others also have much to do with how and when we sleep.

Changing sleep patterns may not be easy, they were not easy for me. Studying about sleep helped me convince myself to get to bed earlier and to buy a good bed. My goal was lights out at 10 and up at 5! I just wanted those quiet early morning hours to luxuriate in slow exercise, meditation and thoughtful, encouraging reading, all of which set a foundation for good energy for the whole day. I could day dream a bit, write a poem if I felt like it and knew that there would be no phone call with problems to solve or distraction from the self formation of peace and joy in my life that morning. Best of all you helped me as I had you at stake. I couldn't suggest a practice to you if I hadn't done it. I also had my strength and energy at stake. I had my peace and joy at stake. So what could motivate you to sleep well?

Good sleep involves first becoming aware of your sleep habits, how they affect your functioning, as well as your eating patterns. Ultimately it means replacing unhealthy sleep habits with healthy alternatives. Like everything else we are doing, it amounts to straightforward common sense practices.

Scheduling. We have already talked about keeping a regular schedule for lights out and waking. We hope you are in sync with those timing issues by now. Please no guilt. Just start again if you aren't there yet. Making new habits takes patience, time and determination. I am counting on you. From now on you are your own sleep monitor.

Oversleeping. Sleep only as much as you need to feel rested. No one else can know how your body functions and your mind works. You have to figure that our yourself. It is suggested that you do not oversleep or spend a lot of time awake in bed, as you want to associate being in bed with wonderful restful sleeping.

About your bed. If your bed does not give you good support, get one that does. Can't afford a new bed? First, ask for it. Then imagine yourself sleeping comfortably and soundly on it. Then keep your eyes open. Here's what happened to me many years ago. I was newly married. My husband and I had a double bed that sagged in the middle. That may sound romantic, but it really wasn't the best for a good nights sleep. Our first solution was to put aside cash for a new bed, sometimes, five dollars, sometimes twenty. We were not rolling in cash at the time but knew if we saved we'd have enough and beds cost a lot less then. This was 45 years ago. About 6 months went by, when one day we were sitting outside on the patio and I glanced over at the side of the house where a large piece of plywood was leaning against the wall and suddenly, my searching mind made the connection. We jumped up and took the board in, slipping it under the mattress and never had a problem again with our sagging mattress! This is not meant to tell you to find stray boards, but to keep your eyes and ears open after you have asked for the new bed....you never know!

About your sheets and covers. Some like flannel sheets and others prefer cotton, smooth percale or silk. If you want to try out different sheets just to see, visit a thrift store. You can buy sheets for two dollars that would cost twenty to fifty dollars or more elsewhere. Same with the fabric and weight of the blanket, comforter, quilt or down comforter. Try out new ones until you are happy. It pays to help make your bed a luscious place to enjoy for 7-9 hours each day. We spend time and money on chairs and sofas and our clothes, why not on our beds?

Preparing your sleep environment. Some healthy actions you might experiment with before you even get in bed to prepare your sleep environment are:

Lowering the light. I turn the light out at 10, so at 9 I make the rounds turning out some lights and turning down others. I turn the bed linens "down" like you would find in a nice hotel or bed and breakfast. The softness of the light helps my mind to slow down. Sometimes I also put a CD on of soft classical music, or meditation music which relaxes me.

Taking a warm bath. Many nights I also get my bath water ready an hour before lights out. A bath with bubbles or soothing oils or a warm shower goes a long way to unwind yourself after a busy day.

Monitoring what you allow into your brain in the hours before sleep. It's best to turn off phone/computer and text messages, unless you are expecting an emergency call. This is also a good time to turn the TV off.

Creating a private space. Stay away from social media late at night. I am not throwing stones at social media. Facebook originated to keep old friends in touch. For me that's what it does. I also use it to send art and writing to friends. However we all know people who use it to advance their issues, opinions and sometimes comments are filled with anger tending on rage that is simply discharged into the ether not even directed at redeeming, meaningful actions. We don't need to take that into our sleep.

Unless there is a life or death emergency, no one really needs to get a hold of us past the time we begin to prepare to sleep. For many people it is just not socially acceptable to call after 9 pm or before 9 am in the morning. That's not a bad rule of thumb. There are always situations that make sense to change that "habit" but generally it is a gift to yourself to have quiet time to honor your own sense of balance in your life.

What else to do during your wind down hour? When we are on a treadmill going fast, we often choose to wind down by slowing our pace. You begin this nightly wind down by lowering lights, preparing the bed, bathing. And If you still are not quite ready for bed, reading is a good idea. That is if it is not work related or something that gets your blood pressure up. Read something light like a magazine, a good novel or just sit relaxed and listen to calm music. I love piano music, a good Native American flute, or music made especially for relaxation.

About eating/drinking before bed. Eating a big meal close to bedtime can disrupt sleep. Best to finish eating 3 to 4 hours before bedtime. If you go to bed at midnight and sleep until 8 am then eating at 8 or 8:30 would not have much effect. For most of us living in the twenty first century, frankly there is no normal time. However, you could probably safely say most people are eating between 5 and 7 pm. If you are changing your lights-out-time to another time, then re-adjust your dinner time to coincide. There are always social occasions that put us eating later. What we are working on here is establishing regular habits for our healthy living, not making rules that allow us to feel guilty when not followed. So be gentle with yourself, as you create your new you.

For years I used to tell people that the caffeine in coffee didn't keep me up. So I'd drink it before bed. I think It gave me the sense that I wasn't tired so I'd head into that next 4 hours from

10-2 pm. Somewhere I'd get drowsy and head to bed. I realize now that it was keeping me up and now generally I don't have caffeine in the evening. Try herb teas or hot water with lemon if you want something warm before bed. Not feeling too well? There's always the old fashion Hot Toddy (brandy/sugar/hot water). But that's off the limit for those of us who stay away from sugar or do not prefer liquor. Some people also drink warm milk before bed.

What does not help are: peanut butter sandwiches, lots of liquid, soft drinks, chocolate, or a whole pint of ice cream!

Meditation: Reading before bed could include: Bible Verses, a Chapter of the Tao Te Ching, your favorite meditation book or a book of quotes for Meditation. Try some of the following suggestions:

"**The Radiance Sutras**" by Loren Roche,

"**To Bless the Space Between Us**" by John O'Donohue

"**Anam Cara**" also by John O'Donohue

"**True Love**": a practice for Awaking the heart by Thich Nhat Hahn

"**The Tao Te Ching**" ed by Stephen Mitchell

"**Sadhana: a** Way to God' by Anthony de Mello (47 meditations)

About exercising before bed: Regular exercise can help you sleep, especially if you can get outdoors and breathe fresh air and are near growing plants and the soothing effects nature has on our bodies. You might try a "nature" locale for your daily walk, which should be up to 25 minutes by this week.

A gentle yoga stretching routine can also be a wonderful way to let go of the fast, sometimes stressful, energies of the day. It could be followed by a shower or luxuriating bath with moisturizing oils added. This end of the day stretching can signal to all those body cells that they can relax now. Walk into the routines you create to make this a rejuvenating time of day. And enjoy your healthy dinner!

About your attitude: Keep a positive association between sleep and your bed. Allow your mind to chase away the negatives.

Find a time, 5 minutes may work well, to go over the days activities. You might want to include a practice of lighting a candle then asking yourself "What occurred that was difficult?" Say a prayer to place a positive response to your reaction to the difficulty. It need not be long. It may amount to releasing a problem that isn't yours to solve or expressing to yourself the knowledge that a solution is there, even if you can't see it now.

Then direct yourself to asking what brought a smile or sense of joy or peace during your day? Sit for a moment of gratitude in that awareness. This is one way you can put to bed those thoughts that keep you up. They will probably get better solved when you allow your body cells to work on the issues while you sleep.

What you do in bed: sleep, not listen to TV or look at Facebook or argue with your spouse or have a long conversation about work or politics from your bed. Enjoy your spouse! Relax..

Start out each day having slept well.
If you do, it will always be "a good hair day"!

WEEK 5

Lesson 23: All the little Cells

Listen to your cells, they are speaking

What are they saying? What do they do? Deepak Chopra says "that having discovered intelligence in the body, it has to come from somewhere, and that may be everywhere."

The brain freely circulates intelligence throughout the body's entire inner space.

"…..With this one discovery, the concept of the intelligent cell took on full-fledged reality." This was published in Chopra's book. ***Quantum Healing*** in 1989. He was stating that "intelligence flows through us." It flows through cells.

Here are some facts about cells.

- There are 37.2 trillion cells in your body
- We think about 300 M cells die every second in our bodies. New ones are born.
- Different cells have different jobs in the body. They eat up fat early in the morning as we have mentioned. They repair all parts of the body. They work as a team! Sometimes they function as an army. They do clean up jobs.
- "A study published on March 20,2014 in the Journal of Neuroscience found that staying awake too long destroys **brain cells** in mice, and may **do** the same in humans. It's the first study to show (if only in animals) that **sleep** loss can lead to irreversible **brain cell damage."** Are you getting your seven hours sleep?
- Cells that do the same job combine together to form **body** tissue, such as muscle, skin, or bone tissue. Groups of different types of **cells** make up the organs in your **body**, such as

your heart, liver, or lungs. Each organ has its own job to **do**, but all organs work together to maintain your **body**.

- "The speed of transmission of a nerve cell is 225 miles per hour, a signal sent from head to toe takes less than 1/50 of a second." Chopra
- Chopra gives many examples of how the intelligence in our bodies operate. P.152
- *Example 1*: "Mozart pulled whole symphonies at a time, not just note by note but as he re-counted the experience, with every orchestral line already composed and orchestrated"
- *Example 2*: "Shauntala Devi, in India multiplied two 13 digit numbers together in her head, arriving at a 23 digit answer in 26 seconds." Try that on.

In "Secrets of Your Cells", biochemist Sondra Barrett puts us in touch with the incredible beauty and organization of the cells of the human body as she translates the small scale life of cells into large scale lessons for living. This is the work of someone with a genuine reverence for the sacredness of Life."

Quoted from Larry Dossey, M.D. author of **Healing Words, Reinventing Medicine** and the **Power of Premonitions"**

Sondra Barrett, PHD wrote a book called **"Secrets of your Cells**": discovering your Body's Inner Intelligence." She speaks of the wisdom of our cells, which are the body's fundamental building blocks. She is a biochemist and university professor who offers programs bridging science, art and the practice of mind-body medicine. She understands the amazing interaction between all aspects of our human life.

She tells several stories about how her cells have spoken to her. The book is definitely a good read. I have my own story to tell that has a similar meaning.

+++++++

Several years ago......we sat in a big room with about 12 tables for 8 and discussed the life of our church community. It was our second meeting and there was a sense that we had made progress. The day was over and people were getting up and moving about. A woman from the other side of the room came toward me and stopped directly in front of me as I rose from my seat.

She said "You should be ashamed of yourself!"

I stood still and said to myself "Breathe"! I slowly took a breath in and then exhaled,

I was watching myself. Then I turned to her and raised my eyebrows and said "Shame"? I paused and then looked straight at her with little expression and said "There is no shame."

I was aware of the negative energy coming from her and slowly began to turn my body away from her. She also turned and walked away.

As I turned I could see a man coming from the opposite side of the room smiling at me.

He was the Bishop's Assistant and had been there during both sessions of our discussions. As I moved toward him, his arms began to raise to hug me. After a big hug, he said "I am so happy you are here at this place." I grinned and we talked of the day's activities.

He was too far away to have heard what the woman said to me or my response. I had not a clue why she thought I should be ashamed. The cells in my body collaborated to rescue me in that strange and fragile moment. A natural response would have been ""Ashamed of what?" which would have put me on the defensive. In retrospect, I could think of nothing at all for which I should be ashamed. I have often wondered what would have happened had I made several assumptions about her words and we had begun an unpleasant relationship then.

What did happen is this: the next time I saw her, she came to give me a hug and five months later she moved to a different part of the country. No one has ever brought up the scene or anything about shame to me.

I am so grateful for the amazing response the intelligence in my cells allowed me to make that day. All I had to do was breathe and wait. I did not premeditate what the "smart" response would be. The words just came spontaneously. It wasn't until afterward that I stood in total amazement at how the scene was played out. It was the play of conscious intelligence orchestrated by a whole symphony of cells that moved my eyebrows up, and encouraged me to be still and say little, neither of which are often my M.O.

The cells seem to say to us, I am right here and connected to your memories, your ability to wait, not talk, to your wisdom and if you just ask for help, we will give it to you.

*I am celebrating the wisdom of my cells
and knowing I have help right here, right now,
anytime I want to pause and breathe and ask for help.*

References

Sondra Barrett, PHD. **Secrets of your cells,** Sounds True. 2013
Deepak Chopra, MD. **Quantum Healing: exploring the frontiers of mind/body medicine,** Bantam Books, 1989

sciencenetlinks.com/student-teacher-sheets/cells-your-body/

WEEK 5

Lesson 24: Water

Water, the elixir of life!!!

Water! Love water, please! It's your friend. Did you know that you could live without food for up to 5 weeks? But, it is said(see ***Elements of Health)***, that life would end in 3-5 days without water. Our bodies are about 70% water. Water is responsible for nearly every bodily process: digestion, absorption, circulation and excretion.

Drop in water content causes decline in blood volume, sodium goes up. We sense thirst and drink a few ounces. Not enough, and we become dehydrated. This happens more when we are older and the weather is hot and we need more water. We can wind up in the hospital, all because we are not taking in enough water.

If you are not paying attention here, let me add a longer list of ailments that can "befriend" you if you do not have adequate water in your system:

Bowel and bladder problems, headaches, anxiety attacks, chronic fatigue syndrome,

muscle aches, damage to kidneys and metabolism, body temperature malfunctioning, excess body fat, poor muscle tone, digestive problems, poor functioning of many organs including the brain, joint and muscle soreness.

Consuming plenty of water can slow the aging process, and prevent or improve arthritis, kidney stones, constipation, arteriosclerosis, obesity, glaucoma, cataracts, diabetes, hypoglycemia, just to name a few.

Along with carbohydrates, proteins and fats, water is one of the four basic nutrients. Water transports waste production and nutrients in and out of cells.

Ok, Ok so how much do I need? We need 8-10 glasses of water a day. You can do it.

There is a place on your menu chart for water to remind you. Eight ounces for one glass! We need 8 to 10 times that or 64 to 80 ounces of water. Does that sound like a lot? It did to me. At first I had trouble trying to drink that much water. Living in Arizona in the summer makes it easier. You rarely see anyone out traveling in the car during an Arizona summer, without several bottles of water available. Also an 8 oz bottle of water is only a cup, one of those very small bottles. Most are 12 to 16 oz. So you don't have to drink 8 or 10 big bottles. Four 16 oz bottles is all you need and you have all day to drink them.

What kinds of water do you usually drink? Find water you like. There is water and then there is water. When a guest comes to my house, I ask if they want water, then I say "I have five options: tap, purified(Brita), regular bottled, Smart Water or sparkling, which would you prefer?"

There are many types of water. Here are some types: tap water, ground water, artesian water, bottled water, mineral water, natural spring water, sparkling water and steam-distilled water. Here is a quick definition of each. Like everything else we are doing, get adventuresome and try out a new kind of water.

Tap water

Because of the concerns due to varying health conditions associated with tap water in different locales, many people are purchasing bottled water. Some areas have water delivered to their homes that is safe and of high quality. The smartest thing to do is check with your water company. Even if you have your own well, you need to have an analysis done of the water.

Ground water: does not come to the surface but must be pumped up

Artesian water: simply means that the water is brought from the ground through a well by natural pressure or flow.

Bottled water: In general bottled water that is meant for human consumption is put into bottles with no additions or sometimes an antimicrobial agent, which must be identified on the label on the bottle. About 25% of the bottled waters sold come from the same source that supply household taps.

Mineral water: most of these are carbonated. The amounts and types of minerals in the water depend upon the source of the water. If you are taking mineral water for minerals you are missing you need to check what minerals are in the bottle. These waters have not less than 250 parts per million of TDS(total dissolved solids). Club soda is called a mineral water because the manufacturer has added bicarbonates, citrates and sodium phosphates to filtered or distilled tap water.

Natural spring water

Water labeled "Natural Spring water" means that the mineral content of the water as it came from the spring is not altered. It comes from underground and flows naturally to the surface and is collected at the spring or through a borehole that feeds the spring.

Warnings are: if you use Spring water for a home water cooler, you should clean the cooler once a month to destroy bacteria.

Sparkling water: This is a healthy alternative to soda and alcoholic drinks but if a flavor is added it can be loaded with sweeteners and is not better than soda pop. Read labels as soda water, seltzer water and tonic water are not considered "bottled waters" but "soft drinks". Some sparkling waters are carbonated from a source other than the one where the water comes from. It is considered "natural" as its mineral content is the same as when it came from the ground. The carbonated water can sometimes be an irritant to the gastrointestinal tract for people suffering from intestinal disorders or ulcers.

*__steam-distilled water__(also called reserve: involves vaporizing the water by steaming it, leaving out most of the bacterial, virus chemicals and minerals and pollutants. The steam is moved to a condensing chamber. It cools there and is condensed to become distilled water. Once you drink it, it operates by leaching inorganic minerals which your cells and the tissues of your body have rejected. The author of "***Elements of Health***" recommend this as "best water" and also suggests to use it in cooking, because "foods such as pasta, rice and beans can absorb chemicals found in non purified water.

It is suggested to add 1-2 Tablespoons of lemon juice or raw apple cider vinegar to add flavor, if desired.

Other Flavored Waters:

And what about flavored waters? Ok to drink waters with flavors, but avoid the ones that have sugar added. Don't like the flavor of artificial sweeteners? Try adding a small amount of natural fruit juice. That still has calories, but is not added sugar. The Washington Post says flavored waters are bad for your teeth. There are choices here to make. Your choices.

The Prize goes to Steam Distilled water!!!
You find that in "Smart Water", sometimes pricer than other choices.

Questions/suggestions:

1. How many cups of water do you drink each day? _____ Do you know?

2. Keep track for the next week and if you are not getting enough water, add "more water" to your list of habits to change. This simply means make a mark on your weekly menu chart for the times you have consumed one 8 once class of water.

3. Remember not to drink anything 3-4 hours before bedtime, to help you get an uninterrupted night's sleep.

4. If you want to "explore" about water, you might try drinking some of the different kinds of water suggested above for a whole week to see how you do.

References

Phyllis A. Balch, CNC **"Prescription for Nutritional Healing,"** 2000 Avery, a division of Penguin Group, Water, pages 35-41

www.washingtonpost.com/water says flavored waters are bad for your teeth.

WEEK 5

Lesson 25: Stressed out?

Allow life to flow the way it will.
Just observe it.

Stress is a major factor in the cause of obesity. You are invited to look carefully at your own life so that you may discover how to change behaviors, actions and thoughts that contribute to your own imbalance. We will encounter the topic of stress in several other lessons. Here is a place to start.

When did we, as a society, start talking about Stress???

It might surprise you to learn that the conception of biological stress is a fairly recent discovery. It wasn't until the late 1950's that endocrinologist Hans Selye first identified and documented stress. While symptoms of stress existed long before Mr. Selye, his discoveries led to new research that has helped millions combat stress.

Definition of stress:

As a verb it means something that creates tension.

As a noun it is "a state of mental or emotional strain or tension resulting from adverse or very demanding circumstances."

Synonyms for stress are: worry, anxiety, trouble, difficulty, hassle, pressure

Stress that's left unchecked can contribute to health problems such
as high blood pressure, heart disease, obesity and diabetes.

symptoms and signs & common effects of stress

On your body...	On your mood...	On your behavior
Headache	Anxiety	Overeating
Muscle tension or pain	Restlessness	Under-eating
Chest pain	Lack of motivation or focus	Angry outbursts
Fatigue	Irritability or anger	Drug or alcohol abuse
Change in sex drive	Sadness	Tobacco use
Stomach upset	Depression	Social withdrawal
Sleep problems		

information from Mayo Clinic

Common Causes of Stress are:

Personal problems:

your health, emotional problems (anger, fear, etc.), relationships, major changes in life, stress in your family or someone else's issues, conflicts with your beliefs and values, assumptions you make.

Social and Job issues:

Your surroundings, your job, your social situation

Post traumatic Stress

Recurring thoughts of a past stress that you have not learned to control

Real Uncontrollable fears: like floods, earthquakes, tsunami's, volcanic eruptions,....a room with walls closing in on you(or is that just 007 and Edgar Allen Poe's poem?)

Learning to name the stress factor's in your life is the first step to controlling it. Please take the time to list below as many stress factors that are impacting your life at this time. Be specific.

Issues of health:

Issues of anger, fear, shame, guilt, or grief:

Changes(or potential changes)of job, residence, financial status etc:

Assumptions, beliefs and fears about global, national or local issues including situations with or about family and friends :

All of these things will change. Your attitude about them will only change when you see them for what they are, do what you can and then release them.

"This too will pass."

Week-End 5

"This (changing habits) isn't a test of your will power. In fact, it is really a surrender of need to control and awakening to the unseen power that is and has always been with you.

It is at last, taking the hand of those who will come to help you and allowing the Universe (God) and the many humans you will encounter on this journey to listen to you, to walk with you, to teach you and to support you. You are not alone."

David Ault

On Changing Habits:

Old habits I am discarding

1.
2.
3.

New habits I am taking on:

1.
2.
3.

Comments about habits I have been working on:

Practices:

25 minutes of walking
Revisioning of old hurts
Preparing a wonderful place for sleep
Are you listening to your cells?
Identifying stressors

WEEK 6

Lesson 26: Popular diets

Yikes! so many popular Diets. How to know what to choose?

Popular diets: While you are loosing weight you probably will be asked about what kind of diet you are following. We know you are changing habits and that is the best answer.

People who bother to ask specifics either want to compare it to what they know about and/or advocate or they may want you to tell them what you are eating. On the other hand they may want you to confess that you just have a tremendous amount of "will power" which, if they are over weight, can absolve them of even the thought of loosing weight because they have already decided they do not have "will power." They know because they have tried and it didn't work. So you might as well be honest and tell them it isn't really will power and it is hard work. The hard work is to change your thinking, which in turn will automatically change your eating habits. Well, almost automatically.

Knowing about some of the most successful weight loss programs will help you to be able to speak knowledgeably to them, as well as to help you walk quietly through the crowd and not get into arguments. What I am advocating here is changing your life style and exchanging unhealthy habits for healthy ones. If you are following, you are learning how to be mindful of your emotions and control them, allow spaces to be peaceful and enough sleep so your body functions optimally for you. You are also learning about foods you need for your health and which ones are less helpful, that your body needs action and stretching as well as rest. But I do not advocate a "Diet Plan". I recommend that you learn how to care for the beautiful and precious body you have been given and then you make the decisions. You are in charge of the outcomes of your life choices.

I'd say the way I strive to eat is more in line with the Mediterranean style eating. I do not think generally that there is a wrong way to eat. The wrong way is the way that does not produce health.

The 9 most popular diets rated by experts in 2017 according to Christian Nordquist and reviewed by Natalie Buter on **medicalnewstoday.com** are listed below. I will make short comments about each.

Atkins diet: focused on controlling the levels of insulin in the body with a low-carb diet composed of protein and fat but low to zero carbs.

The Zone diet: encourages the consumption of high quality carbs and unrefined carbs as olive oil, nuts and avocado.

Ketogenic Diet: used for decades as a treatment of epilepsy, involves reducing carbs and upping fat intake with fats like avocados, coconuts, Brazil nuts, seeds, oily fish and olive oil.

Vegetarian Diet: There are many kinds of vegetarian diets but most do not eat animal based foods, except for eggs, dairy and honey. "studies for the last few years have shown that vegetarians have a lower body weight, suffer less from diseases and typically have a longer life expectancy than those who eat meat."

Vegan Diet: Veganism is more of a way of life and a philosophy than a diet. A vegan does not eat anything that is animal based, including eggs, dairy and honey. They usually choose this diet for environment, ethical and compassionate reasons.

Weight Watchers Diet: is based on loosing weight, exercising and a support network. It was started in 1960 by a homemaker and now has branches all over the world. Participants can join either physically and attend meetings or online. They give lots of support and education.

South Beach Diet: was started in the 1990's by cardiologist Dr Agatson and a nutritionist. Marie Almon. It focuses on control of insulin levels using slow vs fast carbs.

Raw food Diet: involves consuming foods and drinks that are not processed, are completely plant-based and ideally organic. They hold that 3/4 of your food should be uncooked. Many are also vegans, not eating or drinking any animal based products.

Mediterranean Diet: Southern European in origin, it emphasizes eating plant foods, fresh fruits, beans, nuts, whole grain, seeds and olive oil as the main source of dietary fats. Cheese and Yogurt are the main dairy items. It also includes a moderate amount of fish and poultry, up to 4 eggs per week, small amounts of red meat and low to moderate amounts of wine. "up to one third of the Mediterranean Diet consists of fat, with saturated fats not exceeding 8 percent of calorie intake. It is the most extensively studied diet to date, with reliable research supporting its use for improving a person's quality of life and lowering disease risk.

I will add this comment about the most common **General Western diet,** not the ones mentioned above: "Doctor Tasnime Akbaraly from Montpellier, France and team carried out a study that found that the Western style diet which is high in sweet and fried foods, raises a person's risk of dying early. They published their findings in the ***American Journal of Medicine.***"

Reminding you about carbs

Good carbs are: whole grains, fruits, veggies, beans, legumes. They are low in calories, high in nutrient, low in sodium, saturated fat, cholesterol and trans fats.

Bad carbs are: pastries, sodas, processes foods, white rice, white bread. They include corn syrup, white sugar, honey and fruit juices. Bad carbs are high in grains like white flour, low in nutrients and fiber, high in sodium, saturated fat and cholesterol.

So there you have it! Make your custom diet wisely.

WEEK 6

Lesson 27: Clearing old foods

"Get thee behind me!"

Today's word and if you will, task, is about removing temptation, eating healthy foods and being honest with yourself.

You know that if you have that ice cream in the freezer or a fresh loaf of your favorite bread or the left over luscious pie that your family ate last night, but you managed to avoid, and you open the refrig door, it will be smiling at you, blinking eyes, cajoling you, saying "Take me I am yours! Take me!" DON'T DO IT! But sometimes we give in, well maybe you don't because you have "will power". But I do. That's the reason I try to strategize about what food is hanging around my kitchen to tempt me. Today I am asking you to clear out old foods that are out of date or you have come to understand are not healthy for you. This does not need to take a long time. Get a box and a bag. The box is for things you want out of your kitchen. They may be given away. The bag is to throw away things that are outdated, moldy(ugh) or you know aren't good for anyone so you want to throw them.

We have been working hard to live conscious lives, aware of our thoughts, what we say and what we do. We are almost half way through the 12 weeks and it is time to clear out the temptations. If you have items like those I mentioned above and you have a family that isn't following this effort to healthful living, then you have an extra effort of problem solving. You will need to find places for the temptations. If it is in the refrig or freezer, you can find a place under things or a bag to hide the ice cream, push the pie to the back behind the fresh fruit. It's easier to find a special place in the kitchen for the bread. I used to keep mine in a big basket on top of the frig. The sides were so big I couldn't see the contents of the basket. When you get the urge to eat and open that cupboard or refrig door and just stare (oh you don't do that?) then there is nothing so tempt you at first sight. Good!

Axiom One: Out of sight out of mind.

Please stop now and rearrange your biggest refrigerator and fresh food temptations. If you live alone, just don't buy them again. If you have them because you entertained, send them home with someone else.

Clearing the Refrig. Now that you have started the re-arranging, get the box and bag out and clear items from your refrigerator. If there is restaurant food you are "saving" and you haven't eaten it in 3 days, throw. Fresh fruit and veggies older than a week to two, throw. Look at condiments and other items in jars…if you haven't used in a year, throw.

Axiom two: **Get rid of items that are out of date.** Check the expiration date and if it is past, throw or put it in a bin to give away. Don't compromise on quality. The expiration date means the value of the food will lower after that time. Even Worcestershire sauce has a date on it.

Now to the kitchen cupboards! Let's start with the cereals and other things like pasta, crackers etc, as you might be storing those all in the same place. Take the cereals out and check how much sugar they have. The only cereal I know of that has no sugar is Shredded Wheat. Old fashion Post makes it but so does Trader Joe's and a few other of the large chains. Check the contents. I buy granola in the bins where you can purchase by pound, just the amount you want. The one I like best has oats, maple syrup, and nuts. It is caloric due to the nuts and maple syrup, so I have been decreasing how much I buy and I use it in table spoonfuls as a topping.

Axiom Three. **Eliminate items with white flour, high fructose sugar or long lists of preservatives.** If you can, dispose of things made with white flour or high levels of sugar or a label that is 2 inches long with other ingredients they have added to preserve it. Do throw it. There is wheat pasta and there are non-gluten crackers and snacks that are better for you. Dried fruit and nuts are calling to you! You are now taking care of the most precious physical thing you have…your body. Better to feed it the best and have less even if buying the best impacts your wallet.

Axiom Four: **Dispose of what you listed in lesson 3 as "do not like/not good for me** Maybe always, but especially during this time when you are changing habits and loosing weight, do not have food around that is not satisfying to you. Honestly you will feel better without it, just like you will feel when the negative self images are gone. You are making room in your cupboards for healthy foods and plenty of room in your head for happy images.

Please be honest with yourself. Do you want to be healthy? You can't be healthy putting things in your stomach that are not good for you. Continue to learn about your body, digestion, elimination and the many ways your decisions can help those wonderful little cells keep you in top shape.

If you share your home with others who are not eating, or wanting to eat, the way you want to, then you have to say your affirmations regarding your vibrant health more often. You want them to support you, not argue with you. So wait..just wait and loose your weight and love them and they will see what becomes of you and that will turn their hearts and they will believe and be proud of you. They may even decide to join you in being healthy. There is nothing more powerful than experiencing something. You can talk them blue but you need to say nothing, just become healthy. They may have to see materially, but you must see in your imagination, so you can create the new you.

If you are thinking, this will take more time than I have this morning, it may. In that case please get the bag and box out. Then you can take the time the coffee is brewing, or the dishwasher is going or the food is cooking on the stove and start working through your kitchen. It doesn't matter how you do it. It does matter that your cupboards are stocked with fresh food that is good for you.

Have Fun

WEEK 6

Lesson 28: Stress reduction, mind/body support

Stress just seems to happen whether we wish it or want it or don't.

Today's insights about stress are:

- Mind/emotion
- Meditation
- Breathing
- Body Movement/exercise, qigong, yoga, walking

What you have here are tools to help you, after you have identified that stress is lurking near you. Please practice using them today.

Emotion / mind

Are you stressing about the wrong way someone else is acting? or what they have said to you recently? or 25 years ago? It is rather blunt to say it this way, but controlling some else's story, isn't yours to do, even if it is your child, spouse or parent. If it is a full grown adult then you might have to make rational decisions about how much time you spend with them, how much of your love is conditional and methods you can use to avoid having emotions on the rampage. All of this leads to the worse kind of stress, the kind that causes cancer, heart attacks, divorces and death. I mean it's serious.

Training your child before they leave home at 18 **is** your job. And the most effective way to do that is being the example. But you know, because you did it too as a child…that they may not understand or do everything you try to teach them, at first or maybe ever. You can be happy with yourself for having taught them, that was your job. You can hope that before they are a grandparent they might have figured out the value of what you taught them. Meanwhile the only logical response is to let it go before your emotion changes you into a wild roaring beast, which ultimately leaves you at 90 alone in a care home wondering why no one comes to visit you. You have choices. But worry will make you sick and won't solve the problem. Let go of outcomes. Que sera sera.

If you are a perfectionist - Give it up…Just do your best.

Meditation

Focused meditation can do more than anything to help your mind stay on course. We live in a 21st century world that is multitasking all the time and the only way out of chaos is choosing to focus.

We strive to increase our consciousness level understanding that God, the Source of Life is always here inside….. yes?….and also believe that we are a manifestation of love and good in the world, then we just go about doing what we must, to do our part. It sounds easier to think than to do. The many different practices of meditation can help us raise our level of consciousness, so we can at least conceive of living on a higher level and begin to live it.

This always takes us away from the mental/emotional traps, some self made, into which we can easily fall. There are at least 8 different lessons in this workbook that touch on meditation. Our mental participation in the process of healthy living is paramount. Comments and instruction are broken up into smaller parts asking you to do practices during several of the lessons.

One of the most complete books written on Meditation is called ***"The Meditative Mind: the Varieties of Meditative Experience"*** by one of my favorite authors, Daniel Coleman. He gives a survey of 11 different religious paths of Meditation, explains the similarities and differences and deals with the issue of the psychology of meditation.

Breathing

The advice "take a deep breath" holds real truth when it comes to stress. For centuries, Buddhist monks and Hindu yogis have been conscious of the benefits of deliberate breathing especially during meditation.

For an easy 3-5 minute exercise: sit upon your chair with your feet flat on the floor and hands on the tip of your knees. Breathe in and out slowly and deeply concentrating on your lungs and belly as they expand fully. Time with your phone or other timer.

While shallow breathing causes stress, deep breathing oxygenates your blood, helps center your body and clears your mind.

Another time, try counting how many breaths you take in one minute (average is 8-16). Practice slowing it down, slowly taking in the breath and slowly exhaling.

A quite dramatic story of the efficacy of this simple practice comes from the years I served as a Hospice Chaplain. One day I entered the house of a patient to find her husband in a panic. "Oh, I am so glad you are here" he said. "My wife is in a panic and thinks she can't breathe". She was bed bound and hyperventilating quite rapidly. She had a moment when she had difficultly breathing, became frightened, then the rapid breathing, tying to get air, escalated and she had become truly panicked.

I asked her if we could both hold her hand and motioned for the husband to take one hand and I moved to the other side of the bed taking the other hand. I asked them both to count with me. Being the good Minnesotan I am, I counted one Mississippi, two Mississippi, three Mississippi and on. And before you could say Jack Robinson or Jack Rabbit or what ever the saying is…she was calm and smiling at us. And that is how quickly focusing on the breath can calm you. Just remember to say Mississippi in between the numbers!!!

Body Movement

Another quick fix for a stressful situation is movement. Use the stretch exercises mentioned in other lessons. Do the Ballet AM stretch 10 times each movement.

Squats - 10 times. Raised Leg and stretch, each side - 10 times each leg.

Qigong: Raise arms out to side and up to chest height bend in toward you as you raise them and then lower, with palms down as you "sink the Chi". It is grounding the energy. Next, continue stretches with both arms and hands out in front, push out and pull back as you inhale and push out and repeat. Then stretch out to both sides simultaneously, pushing in and out. See the energy is circling inside and around you and you feel better already!

Yoga: lie down and do corpse pose(count to 10 slowly), stand up and hug a tree. If you have a tree near by go out and actually hug the tree paying no attention at all to what the neighbors think. By the time you return to your house the dopamine level that has raised because of your laughter will have greatly, if not entirely, lowered your stress level. It is alright, even healthy, to be silly. If you just can't deal with what other people might think, leave the tree outside unhugged and stand in front of a mirror and practice a dance you remember how to do…the twist or chicken are good or something more updated.

And walking, walking, walking. Just a 10-15 minute walk will clear the air for you, if you can focus on what you are seeing, hearing and experiencing on the walk not on what is stressing you.

By this week you should be walking up to 30 mins a day. A walk of 10 mins will be a synch.

Movement changes
the level and intensity and quality of energy
Move gracefully away from stress

WEEK 6

Lesson 29: The Freedom of Emotional Literacy

"When you know your feelings you know yourself."
The Rev Dr. John W. Downing, MFCC

I met John Downing, who authored the quote above, about a year before I started seminary to study to be an Episcopal priest. He has left this world now, but was an Episcopal priest and a very big help to me. He was also a psychiatrist, one of the ones found on the list we could contact and meet with as a requirement for entering seminary. He informed me that I was emotionally illiterate! We laughed but he was serious and gave me the exercise below to help me get to know my emotions. I don't imagine you are "emotionally illiterate". But it seems we can all do with help to know and control our emotions. Those emotions are both what allow us to experience the best in our lives as well as to lead us down a slippery slope. We have the ability to deal with them by getting to know them.

About the same time I was given this exercise which I have included below for you, I had an experience that really pushed me to using the material he had given me. Honestly, it did change my life, starting with the situation I recount here.

I had invited a 24 year old woman from Nicaragua to come to live with me. She was to spend a year in California working as administrative assistant to our Hispanic Missioner. She was the mother of twins age 4 who were left in Nicaragua under the care of her mother. I was in my late 40's so it "seemed" like she was a daughter. I was so happy for her to be here. I was also involved with Hispanic ministry and we had much fun together.

One evening she went out on a date with a young military man she had met through a friend. She had gone out on dates before and come home by 10 or 11 or so. It got to be 11, then midnight. I wondered where she was and if she was alright. It got to be 1a.m. and then 1:30 a.m. and I was feeling angry that she hadn't called and a few minutes later thinking maybe I should call the hospitals to see if they had brought her in due to an accident. A lot of things rushed through my mind. I realized that I didn't really know what I was feeling and remembered John looking at me saying "you are emotionally illiterate!"

"Ok", I said to myself "Where is that exercise John gave me?" I found it and sat down to do it. Here's what you do

Sit down with a paper and pencil.

- Go through the list (5 pages of emotion words) and write down each feeling that seems to fit you just then. I suggest getting a blank paper and not writing on the "feelings list" so you can have it blank to use the next time.

  Don't stop to reason it out. It is easy to look at all those words and say no, yes, maybe… Maybe I feel that way. If it's a "maybe", write it down to review later..just go through the list writing down what rings true with your feelings with out stopping to analyze.

- After you do that, you may be surprised to see, both many feelings of different intensity and also feelings that are totally opposite.

  When we have opposite feelings at the same time, it's like the colors in a painting are mixed and it looks and feels muddy or murky. We can't really see what reality is. So that is what stops us. We cry without knowing why. We avoid life and sometimes walk absentmindedly into depression.

  We lash out at people. We do lots of things that aren't the best for us or for anyone else. We eat.

- Next, group the feelings and find just a few that best describe the intensity of your feelings. Think about why you feel that way. Maybe a lot of them are related to anger. Other anger related words could be: disappointed, aggressive, rebellious, revengeful, stubborn, impatient, belligerent, argumentative etc.

- If you are able to say to another person or to yourself what you feel and why, it will help you decide what to do with those feelings.

- Sometimes you do not have to "do" anything; just knowing how you feel brings peace.

So back to 1:30 a.m. and Miriam is still not home. I have taken out my list, put things into categories and realize that some are concern (worry) wondering if she if ok. She has never been gone all night. Other emotions are tending to a little anger. She "should be letting me know". She is like a daughter.??? Others about treating her like an adult. Other emotions are around what should I do? Other feelings began to surface. Oh, light just came on. She is a grown woman and a mother. She is not my daughter. She is living in my house but we have never discussed "rules" and I don't even like "rules". And I begin to laugh. Finally I decide to go bed and get some sleep, saying a little prayer that she is ok.

At seven in the morning I hear a Nicaraguan accent in higher than usual tone but loudly say "A-llo. Here I am." I am in the kitchen and I say back, "Good morning Miriam!" I wait a few minutes and walk into her room. She is sitting on the bed and I come and sit down next to her. She starts to apologize for not calling me, but saying everything is ok. She was with Gus. So I look at her and say "How was it?" And smile and she smiles back. "Wonderful she says!"

And time passed. I gave her and Gus a pre-wedding "shower" there at my home. She is now married to him and they have several children. And I do not spend any time wondering how our relationship would have turned out if I hadn't used the "Emotions list." I am just grateful that I did.

I recommend that you use this list to help you see the many different emotions you are feeling all at once. As you get used to doing this you won't need to go to the list. Funny how those same emotions keep surfacing. Get to know them and allow your body and mind to process before you speak or act and life will be more peaceful and productive.

There is no other way more effective to manage your stress than having a handle on your emotions. If you don't who does? Do you give away your life by reacting to other people's anger? stubbornness? or beliefs that you do not agree with? You can manage your emotions. The truth is no one else can. You're it!

Emotional literacy is the first line of defense. Get familiar with your own emotions. The better and more often you can identify them, the more quickly you will see the patterns you play out, time and time again…the same reactions, same emotions, same results, same stop at the grocery store for ice cream!

When you notice the feeling rising, you will first notice it in your body. It may be any of these: head ache, back ache, full feeling, dizzy, shoulders slump down, hands go over the chest…as in fighting mode. Start to notice what you do. That's what feelings are. They are the first notice that your body gives you of danger or something wrong. Feelings are also wonderful. They bring so much joy as well as protection and awareness. We are blessed to have feelings. We just need to get to know them and what to do with them and how to allow them to help us.

It's what our minds do with these first line feelings that is both difficult and freeing. If we are to be free and emotionally literate then we begin to identify the feelings. We give them names and can talk about them. It is then that it seems they are now "emotions" and the names we give them are fraught with layers of both ego and social implication.

An exercise: how you can learn about emotions from your emotions

The exercise at the end of this lesson, that John taught me, will help you to learn to separate the many emotions that you may be feeling all at once and to name them. In all cases you **can** make a difference in how you respond. Some other suggestions for calming an emotional wave are:

- write in your journal
- go for a walk
- head to the bathroom, where you can be alone to collect yourself
- talk to God, Spirit, Universal Intelligence, whatever you call It
- talk directly to Source, as living in your body, asking your body to be calm. Your cells will respond
- practice breathing exercises
- sit still, breathe and allow your emotions to be calm
- they will stop running around and just be still.

Feeling List Exercise. Here again in summary is the exercise I have just been describing to you. It can help you discover and focus on your feelings so you can choose appropriate actions. Next time you find yourself upset, overwhelmed or feeling very strongly, take the list of feelings you find on the next pages:

- Sit down with a paper and pencil.
- Go through the list and write down each feeling that seems to fit you just then.
- After you do that, you may be surprised to see, both many feelings of different intensity and also feelings that are totally opposite.
- Next, group the feelings and find just a few that best describe the intensity of your feelings. Think about why you feel that way.
- If you are able to say to another person what you feel and why, it will help you decide what to do with those feelings.
- Sometimes you do not have to "do" anything; just knowing how you feel brings peace.

This is helpful in identifying your own emotions.

Please do this exercise at least once before the next class.

"The real voyage of discovery consists not in seeking new landscapes but in having new eyes".
Marcel Proust

Emotions list Prepared by John W. Downing 1975

Angry	Beautiful	Cheated	Duped
Anxious	Boggled	Cooperative	Defeated
Antagonistic	Bitchy	Competitive	Deserted
Aggressive	bored	Cornered	Disciplined
Accepted	Brave	Comfortable	Dissolute
Attached	Baited	Clever	Disgusted
Appreciated	Bossy	Contrite	Desirous
Abominable	Benevolent	Crazy	Despised
Arrogant	Bashful	Cramped	Dishonest
Ashamed	Burdened	Clownish	Despondent

Amused

Attentive

Alienated

Apprehensive

Agitated

Apathetic

Ambivalent

Alive

Aware

Argumentative

Aggravated

Amazed

Afraid

Appalled

Authoritative

Affectionate

Agreeable

Alert

Aroused

Adorable

Adequate

Bitter

Beat

Bushed

Belligerent

Beaten

Broke

Blocked

Egotistical

Empty

Expectant

Beautiful

Bright

babied

bold

Belittled

Bewitched

Beautiful

Boisterous

Concerned

Confident

Crushed

Cranky

Closed

Confused

Clean

Calm

Cowardly

Courteous

Cocky

Cheerful

Competent

Composed

Cold

Communicative

Controlled

Courageous

Contented

Crowded

Concentrated

Fortified

Full

Frantic

Convinced

Carefree

Cynical

Compassion

Cantankerous

Cute

Creative

Depressed

Defensive

Dirty

Dependent

Drained

Down

Desired

Demanding

Delighted

Disappointed

Deflated

Defiant

Drunk

Diabolical

Daring

Domineering

Doubtful

Dopey

Doped-up

Despair

Deep

Humble

Helpless

Hysterical

Drowsy

Dizzy

Delirious

Dumb

Devastated

Depleted

Divided

Denied

Disgraced

Dingy

Driven

Discounted

Elated

Ecstatic

Ebullient

Elevated

Elegant

Effective

Exhausted

Envious

Empathetic

Emaciated

Excited

Emancipated

Embarrassed

Exhilarated

Ecstasy

Educated

Impulsive

Interesting

Imprisoned

Energetic

Estranged

Exploited

Expendable

Entranced

Enthusiastic

Enraged

Enhanced

Free

Frightened

Flat

Fantastic

Forgiving

Fat

Foxy

Frustrated

Fearful

Frivolous

Feminine

Failing

Frigid

Fidgety

Fiendish

Flirtatious

Fed-up

Forlorn

Forced

Forgetful

Fitful

Fascinated

Fatigued

Furious

Fragmented

Flexible

Grief

Gross

Gleeful

Gay

Greedy

Glad

Gratitude

Gratified

Grateful

Gloomy

Guilty

Grave

Generous

Gracious

Gallant

Hurt

Happy

Happiness

Healthy

Hopeful

Hungry

Hustled

Hypnotized

Hated

Hateful

Horney

High

Hot

Hurried

Hesitant

Holy

Honored

Horrified

Inadequate

Inflexible

Independent

Ineffective

Indignant

Impressed

Incredulous

Imposed-upon

Infuriated

Irritated

Inspired

Ignored

Interested

Intimate

Irresistible

Intelligent

Inferior

Imaginative

Impotent

Important

Impersonal

Itchy

Ignorant

Indulgent

Inexperienced

Inefficient

Inaccurate

Intent

Intoxicated

Indifferent

Industrious

Impatient

Insecure

Intimidated

Intrigued

Interesting

Jealous

Joyful

Jovial

Kind

Loneliness

Livid

Lascivious

Liberated

Lustful

Loaded

Lively

Love

Loved

Loving

Lukewarm

Loyal

Low

Lonely

Light-headed

Lost

Locked-in

Large

Flabbergast
Friendly
Fierce
Feisty
Flaky

Mad
Manipulated
Morbid
Meek
Mean
Messy
Mournful
Malicious
Moved
Mothered
Moody
Mixed-up
Misused
Mortified
Misled
Miserly
Melancholy
Marvelous
Meditative
Murderous
Mesmerized
Masculine

Nasty
Nebulous
Nauseated
Nervous

Hostile
Hyper
Horrible
Humiliated
Harassed

Overwhelmed
Obnoxious

Pained
Prosperous
Powerful
Panicky
Persistent
Potent
Pressured
Perilous
Poor
Passionate
Pensive
Pity
Pitiful
Paralyzed
Proud
Puky
Privileged
Possessive
Pessimistic
Patronizing
Peaceful
Puzzled
Pushed
Playful

Integrated
Impish
Introverted
Invigorated
Impatient

Pressed
Patriotic

Queasy
Quiet
Queer
Querulous

Rejected
Resilient
Released
Racy
Rushed
Reverent
Ridiculed
Relaxed
Romantic
Rebellious
Ridiculous
Recognized
Refreshed
Rude
Resentful
Regretful
Remorseful
Remiss
Revengeful

Lazy
Lousy
Lethargic

Save
Serene
Suspicious
Sorry
Shocked
Speechless
Searching
Stifled
Smart
Stylish
Sloppy
Small
Stunned
Satisfied
Self-conscious
Satiated
Serious
Sensual
Successful
Sympathetic
Self-righteous
Stilted
Snooty
Silly
Spoiled
Stuck
Stuffy

Non-communicative
Numb
Needy
Negative
Nutty
Naughty
Nonchalant

Optimistic
Odd
Old
Open
Ornery
Oppressed

Sweet
Sleepy

Tingling
Tense
Tall
Terse
Trained
Terrible
Touched
Troubled
Thirstily
Tight
Tranquil
Thankful
Titillated
Triumphant

Passive
Paranoid
Petty
Perplexed
Perverted
Pleased
Provoked
Provocative
Protective
Possessed
Peculiar
Permissive
Pious
Poised

Talkative
Tender
Threatened
Turned-on
Tough
Trusting

Ugly
Up
Used
Unhappy
Unsure
Undernourished
Unrequited
Uncomfortable
Unwanted
Undesirable
Uneasy

Rude
Rich
Resistive
Revolted
Relieved

Sensitive
Shameful
Short
Spaced
Submissive
Seductive
Sentimental
Supportive

Underhanded
Unpopular
Useless
Upset
Up-tight
Unloved
Unnatural
Untidy

Vital
Vicious
Virile
Violent
Vindictive
Vengeful
Vacillating
Vague
Valuable

Stubborn
Sorrowful
Sexy
Selfish
Stimulated
Stark
Stupid
Superior
Self-sufficient
Stoned
Suffocated
Sneaky
Surprised
Smothered

Weak
Wretched
Wild
Withdrawn
Wasted
Wet
Warmth
Well
Weightless
Weary
Wondrous
Weird
Worried

Remember: Thoughts, Values and Feelings are equal but different.

The "process" begins by accurately identifying, totally
    accepting and completely sharing your feelings.
You have a right to all your feelings.
You are responsible for how you act on your feelings.

Feelings change unless they are harbored.
You are not responsible for anyone else's feelings
It is your responsibility to share your feelings with
    significant people in your life.
Blocking, ignoring or denying feelings will lead to
    emotional and physical problems.

AVOID *- "I feel <u>that</u>…" Use instead… "I feel (a feeling word,*
    ex. <u>uneasy</u>) or use, "I think that….." The phase, "I feel
    that is confusing and will only give a thought not a
    feeling.

AVOID *- "I feel like…" Use instead… "I feel (a feeling word,*
    ex. <u>unloved</u>). "I feel like dying." is telling what action
    you are putting on your feeling of "unloved". The phrase
    "I feel like…" is confusing and tells what you would like
    to do about your feeling.
WHEN YOU KNOW YOUR FEELINGS, YOU KNOW
    YOURSELF.

                              The Rev. John W. Downing, MFCC

Lesson 30: Dr. Bieler and moderate fasting

"Thy food shall be thy remedy" Hippocrates

I remember often hearing from my husband, Russ, the story of how his son was healed. His son was a young adult suffering from severe asthma, weak, having gone to doctor after doctor to no avail. Dr. Bieler was well known in the LA area and some of his patients were: Anthony Quinn, Lucille Ball, Greer Garson, Hedda Hopper and Greta Garbo. Dr. Bieler put my step son on a fast of vegetable broth for several weeks, could even have been a month. The son's symptoms all cleared up and he returned to live a healthy life!

This broth consists of 4 vegetables: celery, zucchini, green beans and parsley, cooked lightly in water and for the most part mixed with the water in a blender. Through the years I have consumed "Bieler Broth/veggies" when I felt low energy, various body ailments, aches and pains. When I felt that my body wasn't cooperating, healing or eliminating. I'd go for 3 days and loose weight and get my strength back and I knew that this was better than any medicine. But I never really followed through and allowed the "diet" to cleanse the stomach and intestines and bring new life to me, never until now.

I have a soft spot in my heart for Dr. Bieler and feel that I was led to his book and this way of cleansing and healing. I sometimes think I almost knew him in person. I was living in Laguna Beach and working for Landscape Architects in Dana Point in 1976. One summer we had a big office party at the owners home in Capistrano Beach. It is a beautiful home on the cliffs looking out at the Pacific Ocean with a 180 degree unobstructed view! My boss proudly explained that the previous owner had been a well respected doctor namer Henry Bieler, who wrote a book called ***"Food is Your Best Medicine"***. Dr Bieler lived there in Capistranto Beach at his home from 1954 until his death in 1975 at age 83.

His book is about the conclusions he came to after practicing medicine for 50 years. The most important of those conclusions are his beliefs that:

1. Disease is caused by a toxemia which results in cellular impairment and breakdown, thus paving the way for the multiplication and onslaught of germs.
2. In almost all cases the use of drugs in treating patients is harmful.
3. Disease can be cured through the proper use of correct foods.

His book *"Food is your Best Medicine"* is full of easy to understand explanations of how our body works. At the time of this writing, you can still order a used book for about $2. on amazon.com. This is a real investment in your health. The part I especially want to share with you is the chapter called "Vegetables as Do-It-Yourself Therapy".

He believes that the vegetable kingdom contains our best medicines and recommends alkaline vegetables, cooked, eaten whole or as broth in the water in which they are cooked, alas best without spices. I give in here to salt and pepper and Spike! Again the four vegetables he most often uses together for cleansing and healing are: celery, green beans, zucchini and parsley.

Celery: He says "Did you know that a stalk of celery or a serving of salad greens has more vitamins and minerals than a box of synthetic vitamins."

Green beans: as well as the leafy green plants, are rich in potassium. They supply the alkaline needs of the pancreas and salivary glands which are the body's potassium storehouse

Zucchini: is rich in sodium. For years the Italians used zucchini as a cure-all. "the organic sodium of zucchini, as well as in crook necked squash, is the most ideal source of re-furbishing a sodium exhausted liver."

Parsley: green juices from parsley, spinach and other green leaves can be irritating to an inflamed intestinal lining, so it is best to dilute the juices with distilled water ("Smart Water" is distilled). If they are cooked in water this is accomplished. Parsley is full of Vitamin C.

Hints: steam or cook lightly. overcooking destroys enzymes and vitamins
Use the cooking water for a drink or with the vegetables in a blender as a soup.

Dr Bieler recommended all the foods he promoted because he either personally experienced healing or used them as healing agent with his patients. I have much respect for Dr.Beiler's honest investigations and his courage to sing a different song than has been sung for decades by practicing physicians in this country.

I did not commit myself to the "Bieler Veggies" as I call them, as a regular diet to loose weight or cleanse until I was writing this workbook. I was exercising during the time, continuing to walk 60 minutes, 2 miles a day, did stretch exercises at home and the gym, as well as some qigong and yoga.

I also consumed two or three salads a week and fish, tofu and cottage cheese. Allowing myself a salad meant I could go out for a meal with a friend and still eat. I slowly eased up on coffee, with coffee free days and no bread. The great prize was how great I looked and felt. Wearing smaller clothing sizes after living as a 2X, size 22 person for a good many years, was reward enough! Yes, we can.

About fasting:

Fasting really means abstaining. For some it is only taking in water. I take it as abstaining from something for some time. You may fast from butter or bread and do not eat it for a time. I fasted from cheese and butter once for 5 months to be a partner with a friend who was fasting from cigarettes! I proved I was not addicted and my friend stopped smoking and I never returned to eating much cheese. There are many ways and reasons for fasting. Some are to clean your system, to eliminate foods from your diet, to lose weight in a hurry. I do not recommend long fasts that leave you eating only one thing. I do believe it is good to rest your body from the work of digestion from time to time. Our digestive organs are the largest in our system and need time to replenish to heal our bodies. Do not fast from water, we need water all the time. Some common fasts are:

The lemon Fast: This is found in a small 50 page book called ***"The Master Cleanser"*** by Stanley Burroughs. This man is also full of nutritional wisdom. He recommends the Lemonade Fast, for 10 days and not more than 40. Recipe is : 2 T Lemon or Lime juice, 2 T real Maple Syrup, 1/10 tsp (a dash)of cayenne pepper, water, medium hot…spring water or purified water. It's great and you feel better and will loose weight. If you want to use it more than a few days please read the booklet and talk to your nutritionist.

Broth: A common week-end fast is on chicken, beef or vegetable broth, warm or cold and oranges.The bone **broth diet** (popularized by Dr. Kellyann Petrucci) is a 21-day plan that involves **eating** Paleo for five days and fasting for two.... Many people find that following a Paleo **diet** helps improve symptoms of autoimmune conditions, reduces inflammation, and supports gut health and weight loss. Paleo diet= natural unprocessed foods, fruits, veggies and nuts, avoid dairy and grains, drink a glass of wine a day.

Fruit: Fruit goes through your stomach in about 30 mins(banana longer) so you will not remain feeling full. Go through the list of fruit in Week 2 lesson10 (found in the Appendix) and choose some new fruits along with old favorites and try a 1 or 2 day fast just eating fruit. See how you feel. Don't become a fruitarian. We need balance. Balance makes for healthy bodies, healthy minds, healthy emotions.

Skipping a meal

Eat 2 meals, skip dinner and fast from noon to 7 am the next day. Just to try it on, I challenge you to eat only 1/2 of your dinner two times a week. You will loose more weight and not compromise your health.

Be careful about fasting. Also know there are things your body shouldn't consume to be at best health. For me it is sugar...So I generally fast from sugar. Fast from sodas, and fried food, fast from pizza with gobs of melted cheese, fast from food that makes you feel sluggish and heavy. If you listen and observe, your body will tell you what not to eat!

Bibliography

Bieler, Henry G. MD. *Food is Your Best Medicine*: A doctor discusses the use of proper food instead of drugs to prevent and cure disease Vintage books 1965 (73) 230 pages
Stanley Burroughs, *The Master Cleanser*, Burroughs Books, 1976 (93) 50 pages
Weil, Andrew, MD, *Natural Health, Natural Medicine,* Houghton Mifflin Company, Boston.NewYork, 1995. Pages 203-204

Week-end week 6

Faith is taking the first step, even if you don't see the whole staircase
Martin Luther King Jr.

On Changing Habits:

Old habits I am discarding

1.
2.
3.

New habits I am taking on:

1.
2.
3.

Comments about habits I have been working on:

Practices:

- you are walking 30 minutes this week. You might want to divide into 15 mins am and 15 min pm for your walks
- Start making your own "program" by listing the items you want to eat that are healthy for you in the different food categories by looking at the areas we have addressed. You can complete or add to as we progress through the workbook
- Practice breathing, softly, quietly..time out
- Try the emotion list exercise

Lesson 31: Leafy Greens

It's Leafy Greens Day! Here you have a chance to reinvest in some of the best stuff to eat that helps you be healthy and fills your stomach.

Over the years, I have had to do major habit changes to include leafy greens in my diet. I had nothing against them, they just were not long time friends. I had not been introduced to them much as a child. What we ate in small portions were carrots, corn and peas mixed together in small dishes, with some admonishing that the vegetables were good for us. The salads also were in my mother's small 5" circular dishes. I've come a long way but in a long time. If veggies have not been good friends up until now I ask you to give them a try, speeding up eating them will speed up your increase in health.

Here is a list of leafy greens. Please look through the list and answer the following questions.

1. Which three leafy greens do you. "Love"?

2. Which ones do you avoid?

3. Which ones have you not eaten?

Leafy Green Vegetables

Kale
Collard Greens
Turnip Greens

Swiss chard
Spinach
Mustard Greens
Broccoli
Rapini (Broccoli Rabe):
Red leaf lettuce, Green Leaf lettuce and Romaine lettuce
Cabbage
Bok Choy (and Baby Bok Choy)
Watercress

Green leafy vegetables are a vital source of antioxidants that are the number one food you can eat regularly to help improve your health and boost weight loss. This is because leafy vegetables are full of fiber along with vitamins, minerals, and plant-based substances that help protect you from heart disease, diabetes, and even cancer.

The U.S. Department of Agriculture recommends that adults consume at least three cups of dark green vegetables each week. Really, that is not much!

To those who are eating "raw", of course, eat all of these raw. Most of us are used to cooking many of them, but try them raw too. Try small amounts in your salads, adding nuts, fruit (if you are allowing yourself), sunflower seeds, raisins and cranberries. Fresh fruit like thin sliced apples, sliced strawberries, segments of orange or grapefruit, fresh blueberries are all great. Please go the the Appendix to see the list of Leafy Greens with nutritional content information.

Shopping challenge: Next time you go to the market find all of the leafy greens listed here and see what other ones you can identify. If you are brave…purchase a leafy green that is new to you each week. Look up recipes online and let us know how your experiment was.

References

The Doctor's Book of Food Remedies by Selene Yeager
Prevention Health Books Rodale Press 1998

Online: thescienceofeating.com

Lesson 32: Moving quietly through the crowd

How do you survive for 12 weeks without driving everyone you know crazy as you tell them you can't eat this or you don't to that any more? You move quietly through the crowd, even if the crowd is your family.

As you lose old habits of eating, thinking, behaving, old habits of relating to others and take on new healthier ones, people will notice. They will ask "How did you lose so much weight?" "Why are you smiling all the time? Why? Why? Why?"

The easy answer is changing habits. I am changing habits, all kinds of habits.That's usually enough to say. People ask questions like the grocery clerk who says "how are you today?" They don't expect "I just got served by my wife's attorney and she wants a divorce" or "My mother died this morning" or any number of personal things.

Your close friends and family already know. They have stopped giving you sugary desserts and soda pop. They are scared to death you are going to ask them to go out in the front yard and hug a tree. They worked hard to find an excuse for not signing up with you for the 3k walk next month. And even with all that, they are supporting you.

The dangers of "the crowd" are the arguments, criticisms and suggestions that lead you to derail your commitment to be healthy. They can tigger stress emotions which send you off on a binge or just a pint of ice cream! That's a binge. Sometimes it is their indifference. That's easiest so let's start there.

The Indifferent person You have lost 40 pounds, have a different hair cut and are wearing new clothes which are the epitome of current style! They say "Hi Joe, what's new?" You are thinking "My God, can't you see what's new?" So you are tempted to say "I'm a different person!" If you did they might look at you incredulously with eye brows raised and say "OH?" They don't say more because, like the grocery clerk they are just trying to be polite. You may think they don't really care. Many of them don't. Sometimes they are overweight too and aren't ready to make changes, so they are avoiding being on the defensive themselves by saying little. The danger here is your ego that may have noted that they appear to not really care. Let the alert flag fly, smile do not engage. Ask how they are and move on silently through the crowd.

The pugilist always out for a fight. They pass by and say "Hey what happened you??" Right away they hook you "What happened?" That sounds like fighting words, you think. Why don't they notice how skinny I am, how way cool I am? You are on the defensive before conversation begins. Stop. Breathe. And allow your little cells to respond. If you wait they will tell you what to say. The pugilist says "what happened to you? Your answer "lost some weight, feels good." Try minimalist answers like that. Maybe it's you out for the fight??

The expert sees you at a meeting and gushes at you with compliments and asks how is it that you lost all that weight. The truth is sometimes people just do not notice that a person has lost weight, but are just aware that something is different. Here someone sounds like they really want to know. So you say "Changed habits, that's what it is all about". "What kinds of habits?" you are asked. Then you tell them habits around nutrition, sleep and exercise as well as mental and emotional responses. If you say that it might get a big stare or too many questions for response at a meeting. So a good answer is "I am eating less and exercising more". It's short and simple and gives a specific answer. Changing habits is what it is about, but that's not so easy to talk about or to do! Short and simple allows a response like "That's great Joe, keep it up".

The follower This person really wants to lose weight themselves or has someone close to them who needs to lose a lot of weight. Their face breaks into a broad smile as they say "Oh my Gosh Joan, you look great!" (just what you wanted to hear). The stylish, slimmed down version of you is where I want to be too. What's the secret?" You say "No secret". I've actually lost 40 pounds and changed major habits. She says "What kind of habits?" "Bad habits," you say laughing, "the kind of food I eat, when I eat it, how much. And I have developed some new good habits too… walking and work outs, hanging around with people who also want to be healthy and getting better sleep."

She says "Can I get together with you? My husband and I want to change our lives and stop overeating but we don't really know where to start. We start and stop all the time."

You tell her you'd like to meet with them and suggest a time and place.

And then you become their coach and supporter and together you can make a difference in the level of overweight people there are in the world.

You, your voice When I advise you to move quietly through the crowd, I am thinking of your intentions and wanting to steer you away from conversations and comments that have the potential to derail you and cause stress.

There are a lot of experts out there who will tell you that they have a better way to "get healthy." I believe there are wise choices, but there is not a right way to eat or to live. This workbook is meant to give you the information you need to help you decide what exercise is best for you, what foods bring you health, which ones do not. It is meant for you to experiment with sleep times and mindfully notice the results and choose how much sleep you need, how you can best meditate or focus your mind or how you can relax and play. They are your life choices. It's not a program. It is a guide to give you healthy choices for ways to prevent illness and live a vibrant life.

The other part to 'moving in silence through the crowd' has to do with you, that is your voice be it external or internal. I hope each person in this 12 week course will eventually lose all of his or her excess weight, live long and prosper! I hope you will be an example to as many people as you can, that you will have opportunities to talk about your well-being and continuing health, opportunities to write about it or do videos, to be rich and famous, if you want to be. The truth is people will come to you.

The danger is you will become an expert from your own experience, you will know about the digestive system, your breathing and endurance, about fitness and you will know how to drop habits and form new ones and when you walk through the crowd you will see the other 2/3rd of overweight people and without really thinking, say to yourself things like: He is 30 pounds overweight, she is 80 pounds overweight…or Oh my gosh that whole family is obese. And you will see the person in front of you in the grocery store buying white flour, chocolate chips, 3 boxes of sugary cereals, 4 containers of ice cream and a huge chocolate cake with pink and yellow flowers of sugar on top. You will be tempted to give a lecture. But you won't say anything will you?

You can pause for a moment to envision them at peak health, and smile at them. And it would be best for you to walk quietly through the crowd at that time. We do not like to see people doing harm to themselves, but we do know, because our mothers or grandmothers told us so, that "you can take a horse to water but you can't make him drink"

We can be a manifestation of health and joy and peace
That's what we can do.

WEEK 7

Lesson 33: Off to the gym

Start practicing "Let's go, Let's go!"

Walking into a gym can be terrifying. Really. You see people bent in half over a machine and wonder how they will ever get up again. Then you see a line of ten treadmill machines all filled with skinny people thirty years younger than you, looking like a herd of Greyhounds off to the race.

Oh!!! There's one sensible soul right there in the middle. She's got white hair just like yours only shorter. She must come often. She is watching a TV show and looks like she is walking about 1/2 mile in an hour. She is laughing. Then the TV flickers and the show is over. She takes a long drink of water from a bottle right there in a cubby on the treadmill, monkeys around with the buttons on the machine, whatever they are for.

Your mouth drops. Suddenly she is running up hill on her machine and yelling out "Let's go...Let's go!! You are about to faint and a very handsome 25 year old man comes up to you, introduces himself and asks politely if you'd like a tour of the gym and wonders if you are interested to join. You are thinking "I wonder if he is here every day?" And you say "Sure, I'll take a tour. What's that machine for?" And you are hooked.

On your tour you learn the names of machines and what they do and forget most of it but you notice most people seem to be having fun and the whole place looks safe despite the very strange contraptions some people are using. You notice that you will have to be careful. Some places in the gym seem like a crosswalk on a busy street.

You ask if you join will you able to have a printed sheet with a description of the machines and what they do and how to use them. The handsome dude looks at you with wide open eyes for just a second and then says. "Yes, Mam we can have that for you."

He explains that after you join there will be a more detailed orientation to the equipment and admits that it is a lot to learn and you will want to come back many times to try out all of the machines. You say "How long can we stay at one time"? You notice immediately that you have just said "we" like you have bought into this whole thing. He notices too.

"Oh, Mam," he says smiling. You want to tell him to stop calling you "Mam" because it makes you feel like his great grandmother, which you could be. But your thought is interrupted as he tells you that you will get a key to come and go and they are open all night long.

He also recommends that you don't stay longer than an hour at a time or even less so your body can get used to being used more. And you laugh and think about telling him about the walking program and you are now up to walking 35 minutes every day. Then you change your mind because you have already figured out that some of those people on the treadmill have been running 35 minutes since you came into the gym.

He starts talking about having goals and reaching them every 4-5 weeks and "changing things up" with new exercises and techniques. Your mind is fading and you ask if there is a water fountain. You are drinking the water and looking at this adorable grandson like person and when he says "come on over to my office and we will sign you up" you think. "Ok this is cool. I just joined a gym!" Cool is ok they are still saying that. Then is the easy part. They fill out information on you and you already know from lesson 4 what your BMI is and you are so happy to have a waist not quite so big and you have lost 10 lbs in 7 weeks! You are on a roll. They give you a little piece of plastic on a cord telling you it is a key. It goes over your head and you proudly walk out a new member of the club. You have just given yourself another place where you will find support in your journey to lose part of you and gain the healthy person you see in your self vision.

You vow, that at the end of the 12 week class, you will sign up with a personal trainer and wonder if "he" is available. Oh silly you…you smile as you walk out to your car. On the way home you are remembering that in class the instructor was asking everyone to try to find out what does or would motivate you to loose weight to sign up at a gym. You decide it doesn't matter, you don't know, but you signed up and you are happy about it.

It is better to be aware as we live our lives, but sometimes we just can't get it
and have to depend that our little cells and All-That-Is knows
what kind of motivation works. Then we are just thankful.!!

Silver Sneakers. What is Silver Sneakers?

It's a program that allows you to get health club options for free if you have silver colored hair… white will do. Actually you have to be 65. Many Health insurance companies have an agreement with Silver Sneakers which allows you to be a member and not have to pay for membership in a fitness center.

Medicare Advantage plans, also known as **Medicare** Part C, may provide this benefit. But the regular Plan A and B of Medicare do not cover it. I have United Health Care as my Medicare supplement and have free membership at an Anytime Fitness Gym not far from where I live. The free membership is because I am a member of Silver Sneakers, which I did nothing to join. The membership came with my insurance program. This free membership also allows you to go to classes, yoga, Tai Chi, stretches, Zumba and whatever is offered there. Silver Sneakers has an online store with T-shirts, tanks, hats, fitness equipment and more. So you can wear them and let everyone know you are getting in shape.

Just to make me laugh, I bought a pair of silver sneakers and I wear them to the gym. Do you have "Silver Sneakers'?

Personal fitness trainers can be found at any gym. Some work independently and will come to your home. For those, just make sure you have a reliable reference. The National Strength and Conditioning Association conducted a survey of prices and found an average of $50 per hour with a range of $15 to $100 per hour. I had to pay $75 in Carmel,CA. Prices do vary depending on region and for the most part, they will be higher in urban areas than in rural ones.

What makes a good trainer? To start with, a basic grasp of fitness training. Ask where they were trained? Are they in continuous training to remain a trainer? As long as they know the basics the most important thing is compatibility with you. Do you like each other and respect each other. Are you having fun together. You are not training for the Olympics. But you want someone who believes like you do that you can master your body, loose weight, get tight, walk with confidence, keep your balance and love your body. Don't settle for less.

It is also a good thing if your trainer understands about older fat people loosing weight.

If you are a lot overweight, you will have saggy skin and you want avoid that. The best way to avoid saggy, hanging skin is loose weight slowly and keep moving. It does help if your trainer can create a workout for your arms and legs and around your neck where the wrinkles and sags are most likely to be seen and bother you. Ask what their experience is working with aging clients dealing with sags. If you get a real enterprising trainer and they don't know, they just might be willing to learn in order to help you. Be kind and encourage the trainer.

Online videos

There are lots of online videos, short Youtube videos, 35 minutes, 4 minutes, 2 minutes.

Videos are great but making the effort to get to a gym and work out with other people is good for relationships. The Youtube orientation unfortunately is not able to respond to you.

Best of both: Go to the gym once a week and work out at home for 30-45 minutes 2 times a week. You can do it everyday, of course, but be careful filling your hours with tasks and no time to breathe and just relax. I know over-planning can be dangerous because I do it often and have to weed out the huge growth of projects that prevent my peace to develop. Live in balance.

This week

Stop by a fitness center near you to "check it out" Cost? Do they accept Silver Sneakers? What is available? Pool? Sauna? Self run classes with a screen?

What kind of classes?

My notes_____

_____

_____

_____

Even if you practice at a gym only once a week, but do it consistently, it will make a big difference.

Lesson 34: Clinging

Freedom from Clinging

Those who lose a great deal of weight and change nothing else in their lives, have a good running chance of gaining it all back. It is similar to a long time alcoholic who has partially destroyed his liver, who stops drinking and then returns to drinking, clinging to what is familiar. He or she is in grave danger of a very quick death. So I am told and I have seen with friends.

This workbook is not advocating a loss of weight just to weigh less pounds but to change one's whole lifestyle, to experience a human life of integrated well-being. In following the suggestions during these 3 months you will be changing your life. You are beginning to live differently, think differently and feel differently. We suggest you walk slowly through this change. However the result is a change that can leave you uprooted and without anchor unless you are connected to that which is beyond yourself.

Buddhism has a term called "clinging" that serves to explain what is meant. Michael Singer in his book "the Untethered Soul" speaks elegantly of it in chapter 14 of that book. The chapter is entitled "Letting Go of False Security". What is meant by clinging is the process of attaching to the structure that we build around ourselves to identify who we are.

We work hard most of our lives building up an identity. The we cling to it, even if much of our lives have changed. We may be quiet, soft people who like hiking and do not go out much and have a few good friends. Or perhaps we are the social diva who plans all the parties and knows everyone in town. When we change the habits we have built into our psyche, some of which have to do with food, we can seem off balance to ourselves and definitely off balance to others.

In my twenties and 30's I was a party girl, puffing on cigarettes without inhaling only at parties, drinking scotch "neat"(straight up not even with ice!) only at parties. I was pretty talkative, more likely to be out dancing than home meditating. Well, I wasn't meditating at all. The scotch turned to red wine and two masters degrees turned me into a book person. Now I don't have wine around much at all and soon will not even have coffee and spend most of my time in silence and love every minute of the time I have to paint and write and read! This change has been gradual and people from different parts of my life have seen almost a different person. Some insist that I am the younger me who loves bright colors in my home, in flowers and clothes. But I am not that person any more. Partly I am entering the last years of my life and want a quieter life but I now appreciate the simplicity of minimalism and the serenity of soft muted colors. I am not clinging to who I was. Many people are not blessed with the push to self examine and still want their life the way it always was. The problem is the only constant is change. Nothing ever stays the same.

As you continue to walk into your new life you will discard some habits and take on others. How will friends and family respond when you say you don't drink Pepsi anymore? or do not want the big sugar coated cinnamon rolls "everyone" knew you loved? Even as you consciously make the decision to change much of your outer identity it may still feel disorienting to you and others.

We spend much of our lives creating a persona that is not the real Self. Michael Singer explains the Self as the you that observes you, the you that watches. Many people are so involved in creating the exterior shell that they have not even connected with the inner Self. That Self is the being that remains when the body has dissolved. It is the only one who really knows us and the one who will help us deal with the changes in our lives.

In our state of change we often cling to the definitions of ourselves and our understandings of "our world" that make us feel safe. Without feeling safe we become fearful. Life becomes unbalanced. We cling to habits that are familiar to us just to eliminate the fear. Undertaking this journey to change habits can be very scary. You are more than 1/2 way through the 12 weeks. This is a time to take stock of the changes you've made and plan to make in the next months ahead. If you are not meeting together with others weekly, this is a good time to find a buddy, or ask for a Life Coach to help you maneuver the remaining weeks.

In lesson 32 we discussed "moving through the crowd" to help you deal with social situations. During those times remember to watch what is said as though you were viewing a movie or at the theater, not taking it personally. Be aware of the danger of clinging to those old habits just to create the "comfort" you want. Those feelings that arise when you are not "watching" are also the ones that bring to mind stopping by the grocery to get the pint of ice cream to eat right now before you change your mind. And that is how we slide the slippery slope back down the hill to see-saw dieting and real damage to our bodies.

Watch yourself and others unattached to judgements and outcomes, just observe.

Keep your commitment to the better habits you are developing and adjust them when needed. Free yourself from clinging.

"And all shall be well, and all shall be well,

and all things shall be well"
Dame Julian of Norwich

Reference

Michael Singer, *"The Untethered Soul": the journey beyond yourself,* 2007, New Harbinger Publications, Oakland CA\

WEEK 7

Lesson 35: Alignment

Are you in Alignment?

Our cars get out of alignment, often enough that the tire and car repair places have special prices for tire alignments and expect us to stop in regularly to get an alignment. With the movement of the molten gases beneath the earth and violent or repeated weather conditions, sometimes we even have to get an alignment on our homes. Things shift and change. Roads get cracks in them. We go to the chiropractor for an alignment of our spine. So alignment is not an unusual a term and it is easy to use for our relationship with the power/energy that created us and keeps us filled with the "Elan Vital" (the Creative Force, a term coined by a Frenchman named Bergson), the Source of life.

There are many things that keep us from perfect alignment with Source (Universal Intelligence, God, All-That-Is,) whatever term you use. The term we use is not nearly as important as a shared understanding of what is meant. I like the term Elan Vital because I was a College French major. Sometimes I just say Spirit, meaning Holy Spirit from my Christian background. But I really like the personal connotation of a female figure that is big and beyond understanding but also a friend, so I often just talk to Shakti, a Hindu icon of God who co-created the Universe with Shiva.

One of the biggest things that keeps us out of alignment is our ego that wants everyone to call God what I call God or pray the way I pray or speak as I speak. We start wars, and family feuds and set people and houses on fire, rob them of belongings or love, all because we want them to be the way we think they should be.

We are, every one of us, made differently. Yet we are all a part of this wonderful Creative Force that seems to understand us and bring what we ask for, even if in the end it causes something we think we don't want. That's all It hears..the description of what is not wanted. So be careful of what you ask for. Do you really want "coals of fire" on someone's head?

So the first principle of being in alignment is knowing that there is a Source with which to be aligned. That the Source is the same in every religion in that it is good, kind, compassionate. It is beauty and truth and ever present. All spiritualities hold to this.

None teach that the Essential Spirit is evil.

The second principle is understanding that we are an integral part of that Source and are meant to be in alignment with it. We are part of God. Does that mean that we are God? I am not America but I am an American. I am made of the same stuff as God, for some reason, I surely do not know why, we humans appear to have a larger amount of ability to live in higher levels of consciousness, but we do. It appears that we have the ability to create as does God. In a real sense we live in God, as God. We are one of the manifestations of God, one with higher intelligence. So what does this have to do with me loosing all this weight?

Simply stated: we would not be overweight if we were aligned with Creator and with ourselves. We are reading this material because we want to be aligned with a different vision of ourselves than what we have.

First you need to know that you are not in alignment. We are not made to get so overweight that we lose energy, have to have knee replacements or have a Hoyer lift help up us into and out of a bed. We are are not made to have heart attacks or diabetes.

We are in those conditions or heading there. Our living habits lead us to destinies we do not want. No one else leads us. We have the ability to make choices and be what we want to be. Sometimes our conditions are living habits passed on from generation to generation, but that's not the way the human body was made to be. So we can do what we can to get healthy, then we are aligned with who we are as precious creatures made by God. Then we can use our own energy being kind and compassionate, being beauty and truth and all that is good. When we can do that everything will improve on our earth. The level of Love and Awareness increases just because of one. You know the power of One. We are many, we are legion. We can all be more healthy and help change the direction the world moves making humans extinct by means of illness. Obesity is illness. It is not respecting the holy and beautiful body we have been given.

So, all this Spiritual talk is to help you understand that you are made by that which created all to be a perfect likeness of all that is good, wise, whole and healthy. So that is about being in alignment with the power of God. You are already connected. The alignment is awareness of that connection. But then, are you in alignment with yourself?

Being in alignment with ourselves

For me, living with integrity is living in alignment with myself. If we think we believe something and say it and then do it, we are living in integrity and are in alignment with ourselves.

If we believe that we are made, as humans, to be able to live a noble life, to live, as wise, peaceful, joyful beings…

If we believe that we are able to control our destinies and to be healthy…

If we can admit to ourselves the condition of our body without condemning and not tell others that obesity runs in the family, "that's why we "can't loose weight"…..

If we can walk down those grocery aisles with head held high moving quickly to the fresh fruit and vegetable section, and pass the bakery and frozen desserts and never stop to even look back, then we shall be on our way to victory and what is more, my friend, we shall be living with personal integrity.

BELIEVE IT   SAY IT   DO IT

Week-end week 7

Tell the people in your life how important they are!

On Changing Habits:

Old habits I am discarding

1.
2.
3.

New habits I am taking on:

1.
2.
3.

Comments about habits I have been working on:

Practices:

35 minutes of walking

Move quietly through the crowd as you find fitness centers to check out

Eating leafy greens this week?

Are you in alignment with yourself?

WEEK 8

Lesson 36: Who needs supplements?

"We can protect and strengthen our immunity by eating right, getting enough activity and rest, practicing stress reduction and cultivating healthy emotional states"
Andrew Weil, MD

Honestly there is too much to say about supplements to put in a few pages. So I am answering a few questions that I think you may have in order to introduce you to my plea to become aware of what you eat. That's what I am doing, becoming aware of what I eat. I am having fun learning and am eating with more joy, seeing more energy, watching my body heal. I can not wish any more for you, who are reading this. We don't want to be skinny old people sitting in wheel chairs with teeth falling out wondering how life disappeared, do we? Eating the right foods, full of the nutrition that will keep us whole and laughing until our time to leave, sounds best to me.

What are vitamin supplements?

Sometimes called micronutrients, they are organic substances in foods. They are needed in small amounts to enable specific metabolic reactions. Supplements are not needed if they are supplied in the food you eat.

When do you need vitamins?

- If your diet is inadequate
- If your gastrointestinal absorption mechanisms are impaired, as in hypothyroidism,
- If you are on a special or restricted diet, or taking antibiotics.

Do I need supplements? Yes, if you don't get enough vitamins and minerals in your diet? Maybe not. We live in a world that is in our palm, literally. The tremendous growth of communication during this Age of Technology has brought us face to face with those who want to help us be healthy and those who want to profit from selling fads and those who want to profit from helping us be healthy!

In 1972 the vitamin business in the USA was about $500 Million, by 1988 it increased to $3.5 Billion, in 2015 the market revenue report was $50 Billion with a global estimation of $278.02 Billion by 2024! That's globally, but the U.S. is the largest sector. Vitamin sales have gone global!

What happens if my diet is deficient in necessary vitamins?

You can be treated with therapeutic mega doses of the needed vitamins. Consult a doctor or a nutritionist, don't try to self diagnose. As they say a little knowledge can get you in big trouble,

How do I keep on top of what I am eating and where to find the vitamins I need?

There are several options you have.

- You can begin a self study with this class. As you continue to read about nutrition, pay attention to food and look up vitamin content. Don't have time? or don't want to make time? **or** Just want to know?
- Get a good book on vitamins and healthy living. I suggest Andrew Weil's book called **Natural Health, Natural Medicine"** You can also go online to look for a currently published book. Ask your Primary Care Provider.
- Find a Nutritionist to be on your "healthy you" team. You may want to interview 2 or 3 before you decide who you want to work with. You should be able to make an agreement to meet once a month for a year. Doing that will probably allow you a lower hourly rate. It will also give you continuity, support and accountability. The Nutritionist can be your instructor. That is their specialty. If they don't know the answers you can email your questions and they will learn so they can teach you what you need to know. They will help you plan meals and pay more attention to the food you are eating and the foods you are missing to make a complete healthy diet.

Are you taking supplements?

Which ones? _____

_____

_____

_____

Why? Did someone tell you 20 years ago that you should take something? Have you checked you body systems? What is available now? and what are you are eating or could be eating? Why spend the money on supplements when you could get what you need in delicious whole, organic foods…they taste better than pills.

References

Andrew Weil, MD. **Healthy Aging: a lifelong guide to your Well-being,** Anchor/Random House, 2005. And **Natural Health, Natural Medicine"**

Helene MacLean editor, and DS Thompson, MD consulting Editor. **"Every woman's Health: The complete guide to Body and Mind** by 15 Women Doctors, Prentice Hall, 1980 update 1985.

In the end, no one else is responsible for your health.
You are the one who must decide how to learn and what to learn in order
to take care of the beautiful body given to to you. It is where you live in this life.

WEEK 8

Lesson 37: Proteins

Humans can exist on animal or vegetable protein or both
and be in good health, providing the liver is functioning normally.
Dr Henry Bieler, MD

I was searching for a residential care home for my brother to live in and found one that looked great on paper. They had an opening, so I made an appointment to visit. I explained to the owner that my brother did not eat red meat, and asked if that would be a problem. She paused and hesitated then said "Oh no problem. I guess he could eat eggs every day!" I know that was wrong. He loves Salmon and other fish, and chicken and eats pork. I just said red meat. That was the beginning of my study of proteins and awareness of how many foods have large levels of protein that are plant based as well as from chickens or pigs or other animals and an ocean full of fish and seafoods. I did not know that everything is protein, in some way or another.

What is protein?

Proteins are basic constituents of every living cell and protein is vitally important in our diet. During digestion and assimilation proteins get broken down into their constituent amino acids.

Why do we need it?

The human body cannot grow, develop and repair damage without an adequate supply of the right kind of protein. They form the cells of our bodies, whether they are calcium: the proteins of the bones, or sodium: the protein of the liver, or potassium: protein in the pancreas, the phosphorus proteins in the brain and nerves, the iron and copper proteins of the red blood or the sulphur proteins of the connective tissues. Even the trace elements and vitamins are proteins.

Eating protein can help us lose weight and lower the risk of obesity. Some benefits associated with a good intake of proteins are:

- **Muscle mass:** having enough protein, especially while on a calorie restricted diet is crucial to maintaining muscle mass.
- **Energy expenditure**: studies show that increased protein increases energy output better than any other macronutrient.
- **Satiety:** Protein stays with you longer and therefore can prevent you from eating more, adding more calories and gaining weight.
- **Lower risk of obesity**: replacing carbs and fat with protein can protect you against obesity
- **bone health** "Long term studies show that a high protein intake may improve your bone health."

And how much do we need?

Google says 0.36 grams per day per pound. One study stated 56 grams for a person 156 lbs. If you weigh 140 = about 50 grams. How much are you consuming and how much do you need? Need _____ Consuming _____

Where do we find proteins that are good for loosing weight?

- Seafood and fish (salmon, tuna, mackerel, sardines are also high in Omega 3's)
- poultry(white meat),and eggs
- Milk, cheese and yogurt, cottage cheese
- Beans, peas, peanuts and legumes and soy and Tofu
- Leafy Green veggies and many other veggies
- Lean beef
- avocados and nuts
- Whole grains

What is the best way to eat it?

- Raw or lightly cooked, then it is best tasting and easily digested
- When cooked it should be lightly broiled and rare
- Lamb and beef are the best animal products
- All well cooked proteins are digested with difficulty and produce toxemia especially pork, veal, fish, fowl, small game, sea foods and cheeses. Watch that loaded pizza!

When is too much protein a dangerous thing?

We have here mostly quotes from Dr Bieler's book "**Food is Your Best Medicine**"

- Physically active people need more protein than those of us who are more sedentary.
- Most of us who are very much overweight are not very active physically.
- Eating too much protein is unnatural and may cause harm. Traditional populations got most of their calories from fat or carbs, not protein
- Bieler "if you eat improperly, a good part of your body's activity consists of getting rid of the non food you have fed it. When improper, overcooked proteins are eaten- those which putrefy in the intestine and acidify the liver - a foundation is laid for degenerative disease. This can only end disastrously."
- When excess protein is stored up in the body cells there are unhealthy results.
- "The main source of over acidity is excess protein in the tissues."
- If the liver has to work to neutralize the putrefaction that comes from eating overcooked foods, it is robbed of its' sodium faster than it can be replaced by diet, and as the liver fails, the toxemia increases." My best friend died of liver disease due to inappropriate eating over decades. All of this is closer to home than we like to think.

Choose proteins wisely and increase your strength and vitality!

WEEK 8

Lesson 38: Sugar Addiction

How little is still too Much?

Most of us are addicted to one food or another, chocolate, caffeine, ice cream, choc chip cookies? Sugar looms large as ingredient in many of the items that we are pulled to consume which are not only unhelpful for our health, but actually cause sickness and death. Sugar!! Sweet sugar!

Having discovered Gary Taubes' book called ***"The Case Against Sugar"*** I feel compelled to share some of his information and warnings. This is not just for those of us who struggle with extra weight. His book pertains to our whole society. It addresses one of the major causes of death in our country as well as many other related diseases. If you are going to change only one habit, please make it not eating sugar! Here is what Mr Taubes says in his "author's note"

"The purpose of this book is to present the case against sugar - both **sucrose and high fructose corn syrup** -as the principal cause of the chronic diseases most likely to kill us, or at least accelerate our demise, in the twenty-first century. It's goal is to explain why these sugars are the most likely suspects, and how we arrived at this current situation: a third of all adults are obese, two thirds overweight, almost one in seven is diabetic, and one in four to five will die of cancer; yet the prime suspects for the dietary trigger of these conditions have been, until the last decade, treated as little worse than a source of harmless pleasure."

This is a 300 page book that I suggest you find in the library or purchase online or at a bookstore. It has much more information than I am able to share with you now. Here are a few bullets to help you understand the global situation:

- Most diabetics are Type 2 which associates with overweight and obesity. Type 1 refers to the acute form usually among children. Type 1 kills if untreated far more quickly than Type 2.

- Diabetes is a disease of carbohydrate metabolism that has proven to increase as populations began consuming more sugar

- There was a large increase in sickness after the start of the industrial revolution as people from farms(in US, India … all over the globe) moved to cities and ate the new popular candies, cereal and soft drinks, chocolate bars, ice cream treats.

- "Sugar is uniquely harmful. As a toxin it does its damage over decades.

- This is a well written and informative book. At the end he speaks about how much sugar we should eat,

"Ultimately and obviously, the question of how much is too much becomes a personal decision, just as we as adults, all decide what level of alcohol, caffeine or cigarettes we'll ingest.……Until we try to live without it, until we try to sustain that effort for more than days or just a few weeks, we'll never know"

Over and over you are hearing me suggest that you "try it". Try walking more each day. Try mindfully walking through the grocery store. Try stopping the tsunami of emotion about who-knows-what before it drives you to the ice cream freezer in the store. Try eating without bread, or butter or most cheeses. Try eating more salads and veggies and less meat. Here I am suggesting that you either stop or drastically cut sugar for periods of time, so you can see yourself what it does to your body.

Do some mindful observing around days you are omitting sugar. I do not have sugar in my house. I offer Maple Syrup if people need something sweeter. Maple Syrup does not raise the glucose level as regular white sugar does. It is expensive in calories but does much less harm to your body. I eat yogurt with berries instead of ice cream. I ask for iced tea without sugar. When someone offers me cake or a piece of pie I say "no thank you, I don't eat sugar. Why? Because I feel terrible when I eat sugar, rashes break out and I have a bad after taste in my mouth and it usually affects my elimination the next day. Even if none of that is experienced by you, the cards are in and sugar is killing thousands of people every day and is the major cause of Diabetes and Obesity. Most of us reading this workbook are probably obese. Please stop eating sugar.

Suggestions;

1. Go through your cupboards, find and write down here all the things containing glucose or high fructose cane sugar. Things like raisins don't count. That is natural sugar from the fruit.

2. Go thru your refrigerator and freezer and do the same.

3. Make a list of the top 10 things you consume that you know really are not good for you, like sodas, ice cream, candy bars, sugary cereals, breads, cakes and pies made with sugar. Crying yet? Don't give up. Just decide to break one habit at a time.One at a time. Find substitutes. Look in stores for subs, ask friends.The ideas will come to you and you will be surprised and happy to be eating something delicious that is good for you. An example might be that candy bar with all the choc in your auto glove compartment that is there in case it is two pm and you managed to skip lunch. Make up some small packets of mixed nuts and dried fruits to substitute. Better for you. Such a mixture can be sweet and they don't melt in the car the way chocolate does. There is always a solution.

Item not so good for me   substitute Item

_____

1.
2.
3.
4.

5
6
7
8
9
10

When you go grocery shopping next, read the labels on all the food you buy to see if there is sugar, how much? Is it natural sugar as in Orange or Grapefruit juice or added sugar? and if it is Sucrose or High Fructose Corn Syrup, stay away from the bad stuff.

Reference

Taubes, Gary, *The Case Against Sugar,* Anchor Books (Penguin Random House) 2016

WEEK 8

Lesson 39: Shinrin-Yoku

I feel calmer, more reflective, and refreshed.
I feel like I am taking care of myself
in a way that has a lasting impact."
Rebecca Valentine

Walking for Health

You should be up to walking 30 minutes a day by now, about 1 mile or more. Walking the same route for 6 weeks gets you into a routine. Where ever you have been walking, the habit of daily walking is starting to settle in. Now is the time to branch out to something more exciting. Today's lesson introduces you to Shinrin-Yoku, a nature walk that is now popular in Japan and taking on much interest in the U.S. I hope you are as excited about it as I have been. Some of you may already be going on nature walks and will be happy to learn all of the benefits of such walking.

Shinrin-Yoku, the New Nature Walk

Forest Bathing, is also a name given to this kind of nature walk. The practice began in Japan. Shinrin-yoku simply means taking a short, leisurely visit to a forest for health reasons. You might find that walking in a Japanese Garden would give you the same benefits, but it does not need to be Japanese, it can be in the coastal forests of the West, the mountain forests near you, the Redwood forests, or lovely woods found in so many places of the world, even in city parks of your town, a park only a block away! Many big cities like New York, Los Angeles, San Francisco have dozens of parks easy to access. Google your area and get the overview of big green areas, discover where they are and indulge in forest bathing.

I discovered it in an article from an "Oprah" magazine, written in 2014 by a California woman who went on a 3 hour Shinrin-Yoku in a nearby forest. The walk was guided and focused on what they were seeing, hearing, and smelling. This is a practice that works well to lower stress. If you go for even a shorter time for a stroll in a wooded park you will feel your body relaxing.

Parts of the walk, as described in the article, were silent. Walkers were encouraged to do deep breathing and pay attention to what sparks their senses, like the texture of moss on a tree or bark, the smell of wild flowers. They were asked to notice the beauty in little things like insects on petals of flowers, moss hanging on trees. Notice birds and rabbits, and squirrels and other animals, what they are doing, or not doing.

I have been doing this for quite a few years now, as a part of hiking and photographing nature. This kind of walking takes lots longer because you are watching. You are mindfully allowing yourself to be a part of the forest, to fit silently into its rhythms. You see the play of light, the movement of growing plants, the busy life of insects.

You are distracted from your own thoughts of worry, judgement or fear as you allow your self to become one with nature. It is no wonder that scientific tests show decrease in blood pressure. Tests with the smell of trees also showed decrease in blood pressure.

Not to overwhelm you with test results but these are quite interesting, quotes from Wikipedia: "The smell analysis (olfactory stimulation) was done with the testing of three different tree scents commonly found in Japan. In relation to phytoncides, it is speculated that smells associated with trees/forests would stimulate the most physiological change.[5] The first sample was of Japanese cedar (*Cryptomeria japonica*), which resulted in a decrease both blood pressure and activity in the prefrontal cortext. The second sample was of Hiba (*Thujopsis dolabrata*) oil, which is commonly used to treat anxiety, depression, and kidney dialysis. The results of the test showed that the Hiba oil significantly stimulated the nervous system. The third sample was that of the smell of Taiwan cypress (*Chamaecyparis taiwanensis*), which increased both productivity and concentration. The researchers speculated that the increase in concentration was due to relaxation caused by the Taiwan cypress essential oil.

There have also been tests of people taking a regular 20 min walk in a forest and others walking in a crowded urban setting. The subjects showed a much lower hemoglobin concentration, an increase in concentration and lowered stress hormones when they were walking in the forest. Tests in Japan have shown that diabetic patients have been able to lower glucose levels as far as 40% for walks between 2-4 miles! By the end of our 12 weeks you will be walking at least 2 miles daily. Think it's worth the effort?

Just in case you are sloughing off on walking...really it is the easiest thing you can do to improve your heath, except getting a good nights sleep! And no, for an hour's walk you don't need those chocolate protein bars!

Psychological effects show that forest environments have been found to be advantageous with respect to acute emotions, especially among those experiencing chronic stress.

Other tests mentioned in the magazine article stated the lowering of cortisol, the stress hormone, by almost 16 percent. "One of the biggest benefits may come from breathing in chemicals called phytoncides, emitted by trees and plants. Women who logged 2 to 4 hours in a forest on 2 consecutive days saw a nearly 40 percent surge in the activity of cancer fighting white blood cells, according to one study. "Phytoncide exposure reduces stress hormones and indirectly increases the immune systems ability to kill tumor cells" says Tokyo based researcher Qing Li,MD,PHD, who has studied Shinrin-Yoku.

Mindfulness and spending time in nature both have restorative properties of their own, add building strength and muscle, add enjoying the beauty of nature, a chance to find a calm space and time to be reflective, and the knowledge that you are doing something to build a healthier you without spending money, all of that should bring a big smile and sense of satisfaction. That satisfaction is hard to find sometimes in our fast paced world. It's too easy. Like the best things in life. The peace and joy of a forest bath is very close to you and very available. Ask for it and you will receive it. Ask Google where!

Questions

1. Are you up to 40 mins a day this week? yes, congratulations! no? what prevents the walking? _____

_____

Do you need someone to walk with you to be accountable? _____ if so, ask for one to come into your life. They will come. Go with them.

Practices:

1. Locate the wooded areas near where you live, or peaceful locations near water or mountains.

2. Make a date with yourself to go for a Shrin-yoku experience for at least 30 mins in the next week to 10 days

3. If you liked it, go again and take a friend.

References:

Oprah Magazine June 2014 page 92 "The New Nature Walk by Nicole Frehsee.

Wikipedia article on Forest Bathing

Lesson 40: Creating the new you

Your part in creating the healthy, slim you is summarized here.

Clarify outcome
Know your Source
Know your part of Source
Envision the outcome.
Feel the gratitude.
Allow it to happen

Clarify outcome: Get specific about what you want to create. In a sense you have already done that when you set your goal. It helps if you can articulate why you want to loose the weight. What about your situation needs to change? This is where you can list the negatives.

_____

_____

_____

Here we are going through the most effective way to get to your goal. Clarify what you want first…then ask and receive.

Know the source of your power to achieve your goal: Last week we talked about being in alignment with God/Source. People say to me "you must have had a lot of will power!" I never thought it was "will power". Maybe it has been motivation, but more knowing I'd have the backing to do it, the courage, when things were slow or I got thinking about being ugly, fat, unloveable. During the years I was loosing the weight many things motivated me; the romance, the job I wanted to have, the friend who was loosing weight, just plain self disgust, the amazing thought that I could do it.

I'd say a prayer to lose weight and go off and eat that Talenti gelato when my emotions got stirred. What happened for me is the awareness that I can ask and God really does answer prayer!

Know that you are a part of Source: I also became aware that I am a part of God, part of the prayer and the intuitive knowledge that God is working through me, for me, as me. I learned to listen better to that inner voice that spoke the kind words telling me that I was beautiful and whole and healthy. That's what in the end could cajole me into sticking with it. So that part of it was not just knowing there was an omnipotent being. It was knowing that being was in me and wanted to act as me and show others that we are beautiful and whole.

See the outcome: I was told in seminary that I have a large imagination that only about 3% of the population have. Honestly I took it as a compliment! I met someone who told me that her father had impressed upon her that it was evil to imagine things. Also I had a very good friend who could not ever, over a 60 year friendship, imagine what kind of life she wanted to live. I do feel blessed by my imagination but the truth is…we all have imaginations. So if yours is in hibernation please get it out and start practicing.

I do think you will need to have a vision of you at ideal weight. Your effort to make a "Beautiful Me Binder" is part of your visioning. It is good to see actual images. But I would like to encourage you to every day find something that pushes that imagine into your mind. It could be in a magazine you are looking at while you are waiting somewhere, a clothing catalogue that comes to your house, a stranger passing by that makes you want to say "That's how good I will look in my clothes'" or "I'll play tennis like that! "Or Swim or dance like that!

A sober note is: If you can't imagine yourself at goal weight and healthy, chances are you won't get there. Your own power to envision is a huge part of how you use your power to create. You see it. You see it and walk by the pastry shop because what you see is worth more than the instant gratification of whatever is tempting you.

Jot down a few words to remind yourself of the vision of you at goal weight, what you look like, what you can do that you can't now, how you will feel about yourself. What difference will it make?

_____

_____

_____

_____

_____

Be thankful: Part of your work to create a new healthy life is your gratitude. You will not do it alone. Thank all the people who are helping you. Hold up their dreams so they may have your energy to help them. Look in the mirror and be thankful that you can finally see the bone structure in your face, walk an hour without huffing and puffing and fit into a smaller size. Thank yourself for persisting and believing in yourself

Write down here the names of people who are helping you, believing in you. Don't forget add you.

Release your desire allowing what you need to come to you. The truth is you do not need to do this alone. People will appear, ideas in your head will appear, there will be someone to walk with and talk with as you go. But don't fret or worry. Envision and trust and be thankful. I am so thankful. Be thankful before you reach your ideal weight. Allow it to come to you.

You can use this process to change any situation in your life and create something new. What needs to be understood is you are asking and you will be given. You will be given what you ask for and you will be a part of it happening. But you do not need to make the complete 5 year plan, with objectives and action plans. Ask and wait to see how it unfolds. Don't say what you don't want because that's probably what you will get. And try hard not to ask for 2 opposite things because that is a very confusing order to fill. However, Source (God) will be busy connecting the dots and bringing what you need. Your part is to stay aware so you see what is coming your way. What stops it is not believing it will happen, and not allowing it to happen.

Try it and you will see

Week 8 Week-end

We can each create our own dance and still stay with the music.

Chaos and order coexist in divine harmony.

I give thanks for the lines, even if I color outside of them.

Rev Katherine. Saux

On Changing Habits:

Old habits I am discarding

1.
2.
3.

New habits I am taking on:

1.
2.
3.

Comments about habits I have been working on:

Practices:

40 minutes you are walking. 20 minutes a.m. and 20 minutes p.m.?

Avoid sugar

Run to nature and bathe in it!

Hug a tree

Dance your dance

Move quietly through the crowd as you find fitness centers to check out

Eating leafy greens this week?

Are you in alignment with yourself?

WEEK 9

Lesson 41: Stress Support

One of the most important actions is waiting.

Let's take time today to think about how we can help each other in stressful situations. We can ask for help from others. We can look for safe people to support us and we can support ourselves by going within to meet our own strength. Here are some things to ponder today.

Accountability: partner/confidant/supporter/coach

- Call a friend and talk about your issues.
- Good relationships with friends and loved ones are important for a healthy life style.
- A reassuring voice, even for a minute, can put everything in perspective.
- Call your Life Coach or make a note about what to discuss next time you meet.

Safe and Unsafe people

- Is the person you call safe?
- Will they guard your emotions and respect them?
- Will they listen?
- When you see they don't listen, stop. Just ease out of the conversation.
- You don't need to lose them as a friend. They just may not be the person to listen for now. This is usually because of their own issues, or their listening skills are not well honed, or they are having a bad hair day.
- Call another friend who will listen respectfully.

Self Support

Sometimes calling a friend is not an option. In that case, talk yourself through it.

I usually do that by writing in my journal to a friend who turns out to be the Holy Spirit/Shakti. She always answers me. She takes a non-judgmental observer view point. Wisdom really does reside inside. And she gives better answers than most human friends.

Tell yourself why you are stressed out. Journal if you can. Ask yourself questions and be honest in answering. Work out what you need to do to deal with the task at hand. List options. And most importantly, assure yourself that things will change, that everything will work out the way it is supposed to. "This too shall pass." We don't always have the answers but we have the questions.

We need to have at our fingertips the actions that will allow our minds and hearts to act together for our highest good. One of the most important actions is waiting. Think of the Buddha sitting under the tree. Just be still and allow your intuition to connect to Source/God. Trust that awareness of the right action will come when it is time. Just be still and know.

Most of the stress that lingers with us and does damage comes from our own holding on to emotions that are not helpful or even realistic. Our minds figure it out but our emotions are strong and just take control sometimes. I share a poem about allowing the heart/emotions and mind to walk together, with the wish for you that you may allow them to enjoy your life together.

The Meeting

They walked on parallel paths for years
One knew
One searched
One accepted
One investigated.

There were times when their paths merged
and for miles they walked together in harmony,

content. Unfettered joy gave easy steps
along the journey.

Then back to the banter of why and what if
and the fear that always made them choose
to walk again on parallel paths.

Perhaps some day these two, mind and heart
will see that they are formed together to act
as one and shall then find a path
that brings the fulfillment
each has longed for, all these years.

It's not what someone else says or does that makes stress in our lives. It is what we do with it. When our heart/emotion and mind work together we have healthy results.

Take time out so that the stress level does not build up to high pressure. Take "me time". Take time for you alone, anything from a sauna to a walk in nature, to a trip, to a gallery or shopping. Take some "me time" every day.

Vacations:

Weekly: take time off from work and/or whatever is causing stress.

Monthly: plan a time to have fun, learn something new, go to a movie, invite a friend over.

Yearly: Plan your vacation time, include a week, at least enough time to relax. If you can, arrange 3 times a year for mini vacations. Put them on your calendar.

> ***Take yourself to a peaceful place,***
> ***even if it is in your imagination.***

Lesson 42: Clearing the Mind

Learn to Focus

A big part of loosing old habits and making new ones centers in our self awareness. A meditation practice can be what helps us center and see our world in a detached, non judgmental way. Do you have an experience with Zen Buddhism? with zazen? which is a Japanese word meaning insight or mindfulness? If you do, this is a bit of a review, if not, then listen and you shall hear.

Zen Meditation is more something you do than study about. It is a practice. I was introduced to it in August of 2007 when I choose to attend a 5 day Sesshin. It was a silent retreat at the Redemptorist Center in Tucson, AZ. We ate in silence, sat in silence and walked together in silence. We all stayed overnight in our own rooms at the retreat center and were asked not to chat with each other. During the meals we took turns helping to set the table, clear the dishes and wash them, only speaking to ask a question or give direction. We were asked to wear clothes of dark colors without flashy designs on them so as to not be distracting. There were 20 of us. No one was Japanese or Asian. Where we all came from or what we did for a living, I never knew. Despite lack of a cozy buddy-like 5 days together, I must tell you I have never felt a sense of deep community as much as I did during those 5 days!

We all knew that we were there to practice stilling our minds, focusing and not making judgements of each other or even ourselves. During our "sitting" time together we were in a room that was called the Zendo. It mostly had cushions on the sides of the room. There were folding chairs if we preferred. At the beginning only three of us had chairs but by the end there were 7 chairs! The room has a wonderful view of the desert and is cool to help prevent you from falling asleep. There was a table, next to the leader's chair at the end of the room with candles lit and incense burning. It was very peaceful.

We sat for 25 minute sessions in silence facing the wall, then at the sound of a gong all rose and walked, turning to the left to follow the person next to us and walked for 10-15 minutes. After the initial 25 minutes of silence, which I was not used to, I couldn't wait to get up and take some long strides to stretch my legs. I am a hiker and was picturing walking the grounds, taking deep breaths and enjoying the scenery. The gong sounded. We all arose, turned to bow and face the center, then turned to our left. The leader led us in walking, one after another. We were to take a breath in as we moved the right foot forward and exhale the air as we moved the left foot. I almost laughed out loud. So different from my vision of a stroll in the desert! We got to see lots of bare feet and several times on our path met a tarantula which we gently stepped over.

This is really where I learned to focus. Mostly people focus for a few seconds and are on to another thought, another station on TV. Most of us have trouble even listening to a friend talk if they are talking slowly or not holding our interest. TV commercials are quick, never more than 30 seconds...Even red/green lights at the intersection. Have you ever counted the time it takes to change lights? Usually 15 seconds for secondary streets and about 30 to sometimes 40 seconds at major intersections. So this world of extended quiet was different, scary at first and then became the practice I most treasure.

Zazen, or sitting in Zen style is a practice 5,000 years old from India and has been brought to us in the US through Japanese Zen Buddhism. However, it is, in one form or another, present in most spiritualities around the globe.

It is a habit that will

- Help you to allow you heart and mind to walk together
- Cause you to listen better to others rather than react
- Help you make better decisions about when you sleep, when and what you eat and how you choose to keep your body fit

The more fit your body is the easier it is to sit for 25 minutes or 30 or 45!
And you might even get to sitting cross legged on cushions!

You can join groups or read books that tell you to hold your breath or follow some precepts from one stage to another or join a system planned by someone else.

Or you can just sit and clear your mind.

If you find a Zen center near you, you might want to join them for a time to practice together until it becomes a habit. There you will also have others to ask for advice who will not try to tell you that you need to be a Buddhist or give up whatever spiritual organization you belong to.

To quote Daniel Coleman from "the Meditative Mind" (p. 89) on zen sitting:

""just sitting": In any type of Zen meditation, the student marshals a heightened state of awareness with no primary object. He just sits, keenly aware of whatever goes on in and around him. He sits alert and mindful, free from points of view or discriminating thoughts, merely watching."

And to encourage you, I add another quote. Below Coleman is quoting from Ruth Sasaki:

> "The experienced practitioner of zazen does not depend upon sitting in quietude on his cushion. States of consciousness at first only attained in the meditation hall gradually become continuous, regardless of what other activities in which she may be engaged."

Take care of your mind, dear ones.
Help your intuition to train your mind to be still and know.

Lesson 43: Minimalistic Eating

"Less is More"

We know some responses to questions about how we lost our weight. The most comprehensive is changing habits. But if you get tired of saying that, you can say it's all about minimalism.

Minimalism, yikes what's that? I thought it was an art movement. Yes, it is. It was Ludwig Mies Van Der Rohe, an architect, who first made it popular as a precept for minimalist furniture design and architecture. It is an art movement that began post World War II in Western art, most strongly in the visual arts in the 1960's and early '70's. It is like a Japanese Haiku, using the fewest words to say something meaningful. In our homes it may be lack of clutter, emptying spaces that were too crowded. It is a vase sitting on a table with only a few beautiful flowers, not a mass bouquet of mixed colors and types.

Our process of losing weight and forming a new life, is also about cleaning out and clearing spaces so the basic beauty can be seen. You are the basic beauty. Some of the things we are clearing out are:

- our cupboards, refrig and freezer of foods that no longer serve a healthy body
- our closets of old clothes that don't fit us anymore or we don't wear because we just aren't the same old person anymore
- our minds of old stories of how unloveable we are, how fat, what a mess we are
- our ideas that always bring us to "I can't"….I can't fit into the airplane seat, I can't walk that far, I don't have enough energy

Minimalism is a concept I have used many times in many ways during my own process of "losing me". We really do not need to eat the amount of food most of us have been used to eating and is served at most restaurants. Here are some ideas:

Use smaller plates. A normal dinner plate is 10" wide, a luncheon plate is 9" wide and a salad or desert plate is 7.5 to 8" wide. The plates I normally use for my food are 7" wide. I use a shallow bowl for salads and also use it for cooked veggies with a piece of fish on top. They are 9" wide but the interior sloping inward is about 6 inches wide. I never have a full 10" plate unless half of it is salad.

Use smaller glasses for everything you drink except water. Use bigger ones for water! No, you don't have to buy a new set of dishes. Ask around about where the thrift stores are and get one plate or one glass or two.

Take smaller portions: A very wise woman, who worked with 2 men who were big eaters and often went out for breakfast meetings with them, commented to me that they really didn't need 2 eggs, they could have just ordered one. I took that as a hint and many times I only have one egg. I know people whose habit includes eating 3 at a time. Not really so good for cholesterol! How about 2 strips of bacon instead of three, no butter on the pancakes just syrup. There is a lot of nutritional wisdom that says you had best not be eating any of those things. If you are beginning to change your habits. Start where you can.

Out for a meal: Bring home half. I find most times that half is enough for another meal. One trick is to ask the waiter, right off for a take-home box and divide the meal in two so you don't sit there picking at it until it is gone, even though half way through the meal you felt satiated.

Have a bite: If you are eating out at a home or a restaurant and want to resist the meal that will be too rich or the desert that has the forbidden sugar, ask whoever is eating it for a bite. Savor it like a real gourmet and smile inwardly that you did not succumb to acting the gourmand and stuffing yourself.

2 meals a day: Eat a late breakfast and an early dinner and add a piece of fruit later before 7 p.m. This will basically mean eating two meals instead of three. I try to eat my three mini meals, but sometimes want a "big old breakfast", or a brunch. It's good to change routines. We are breaking bad habits for better ones. However, not being able to change habits makes us less resilient and often cranky when we get "old" and insist that "it's my way or no way." As you change make sure sure you build in resiliency.

Applying minimalism to our daily choices can sometimes be a stretch and difficult but you are setting an example for others, who may go home and say "if Sally can, so can I!"

Be brave and think of something
every day this week that you can do less.

WEEK 9

Lesson 44: Carbohydrates

"Best sources of fiber are: fruits, whole grains
and vegetables, especially legumes."
Dr Andrew Weil, MD in *Natural Health Natural Medicine*

Definition of Carbohydrates: any of a large group of organic compounds occurring in foods and living tissues and including sugars, starch and cellulose.

What Carbohydrates do in our bodies and why we need them:

At the chemical level these foods contain carbon, hydrogen and oxygen, thus the name carbohydrates. They are one of the three main ways our bodies contain calories or energy. The other two are proteins and fat. Carbs are the sugars, starches and fibers we get from fruit, grains, vegetable and milk products.

Ways carbs function in our bodies:

*   provide fuel for the central nervous system
*   enable fat metabolism
*   help our brains function
*   provide a quick energy source, dopamine levels increase after eating carbs

Complex and Simple carbs have different chemical structures and different rates that sugar is absorbed and digested.

Simple carbs are digested more quickly and easily. Examples are milk and fruits.

They are also found in candy, soda and syrups, as they do not have vitamins or fiber they are said to have "empty calories" and lead, you guessed it, to weight gain. They can cause bursts of energy, more so than complex carbs because of the quicker rate at which they are absorbed.

Complex carbs have 3 or more sugars, often called starchy foods. Examples are: beans, peas, lentils, peanuts, potatoes, corn, parsnips, whole grain breads and cereals. These carbs lead to a more stable energy. Most agree that whole grains and veggies will give you a longer lasting sense of well-being.

Sugars, starches and fibers: Carbs are broken down into smaller units of sugar, as glucose and fructose. They are absorbed by the small intestine and sent through the blood steam to the liver, where the sugars are converted to glucose, again entering the blood stream, along with insulin and finally converted to energy for us to function. Our amazing intricate bodies!

Fiber: We need fiber to digest our food, have healthy bowel movements and prevent diseases such as heart and diabetes (says US Department of Agriculture). Unlike sugars and starches, fibers by-pass the small intestine and are digested in the large intestine, where they are converted to hydrogen and carbon dioxide and fatty cells. The Institute of Medicine recommends 14 grams of fiber for every 1,000 calories consumed. Dr Andrew Weil suggests we should be eating about 40 grams of fiber daily, about twice the amount we eat. Best sources of fiber are: fruits, grains and vegetables, especially legumes. They are also found in non-starchy vegetables like: lettuces, kale, green beans, celery, carrots and broccoli.

Carbohydrates are good for you! the right kind. They are good for your mental health, for weight loss, nutrients, and heart health. Without good carbs you lose energy.

The recommended daily amount (RDA) of carbs for adults is 135 grams, according to the National Institute of Health. This may vary depending upon your age, fitness and body size. Intake should be between 45 to 65 percent of total calories. Consult a nutritionist or Preventative Medicine Doctor if you have irregular circumstances. Consult anyway.

Good and bad carbs

Good = complex carbs as in whole grains, fruits, veggies, beans, legumes.

According to Pritikin Longevity Center they are: low in calories, high in nutrients, without refined sugar or grains, high in natural fiber, low in sodium, low in saturated fat, low or devoid of cholesterol and trans fats.

Bad = pastries, sodas, processed foods, white rice, white bread. They are high in calories. They are found in refined sugars like corn syrup, white sugar, honey and fruit juices and are high in grains like white flour, low in nutrients and fiber, high in sodium, saturated fat and cholesterol.

Some **"superfoods"** are leafy greens (you already know from lesson 31), sweet potatoes, citruses, apples and whole grains are good. Here are more carb foods good for weight loss:

Oatmeal is high in soluble fiber, which means that it dissolves slowly after you eat, keeping you sustained for much longer than, say, crispy rice cereal. Plus, food studies link oatmeal to blasting visceral fat, which is the hard to combat fat that sits around your mid-section and your vital organs (as your heart!).

Vegetables: You probably didn't think vegetables were in the carbohydrate category when you ousted them from your diet plans. However, these colorful carbohydrates contain the essential fiber, vitamins, minerals, and antioxidants needed to fight free radical damage as well as weight gain, cancer, and many other harmful diseases.

Fruit: Like veggies, fruits are often overlooked in the carbohydrate category. However, these naturally sweet, healthy carbs are rich in fiber, as well as a plethora of vitamins, minerals and antioxidants. They're healthy and they satisfy those sugar cravings.

Beans, beans are good for your heart! And yes, the more you eat, the more regular your digestive system will function, which aids greatly in weight loss. Plus, in addition to being high in fiber, beans also pack valuable amounts of protein and iron to fuel your workouts.

Other excellent foods, less used by the larger population are: bulgar wheat, wheat berries, quinoa, whole grain pasta, brown rice, and barley.

Carbs to avoid: you know really....ice cream, popcorn, doughnuts, pancakes, white bread, white rice and white potatoes, cake, pie and so on. Once you get used to not eating them and feel healthy, you will not want them. Try, you'll see. But just in case you are struggling, something that helps is looking up how some foods are made and of what and what that does to your body. Really, big chunks of melted cheese with meat on white bread pizza .....actually has been the last straw leading up to a heart attack for some of my friends! You are the one those cells are counting on. You are the General giving the orders. Give your cells a chance to keep you healthy.

We need carbohydrates but carbs are sometimes stored in the body(as fat). "The fat deposits could be viewed as a type of carbohydrate bank, where deposit and withdrawals are made as necessary." (*Fit for Life* p.96) Do eat carbs but not in excess, if your body needs more it will reduce you by making a withdrawal of the stored fat. Just don't take too much out at one time.

This is really not a workbook about body chemistry. However, if you are interested, if it will help you understand why you should eat some things and avoid others, I suggest reading chapter 5 (Digestion: first line of Defense against Disease) in Dr. Henry Bieler's book "*Food is your Best Medicine*".

Suggestions/questions

1. List 5 good and 5 bad carbohydrates you often consume:

2. Do you need to make changes in this area? _____ Doing ok?_____

3. Some new carb foods you are willing to try are: _____

References

activebeat.com

Diamond, Harvey and Marilyn, ***Fit for Life*** 1985 Warner Books

livescience.com 2017 an article by Jessie Szalay, Live Science Contributor

Bieler, Henry G, MD, ***"Food is your Best Medicine"*** 1965 Vintage Books

Weil, Andrew, MD ***"Natural Health, Natural Medicine"*** 1995 Houghton, Mifflin

WEEK 9

Lesson 45: Insomnia

"A surprisingly simple set of rules can solve most cases of insomnia."
Professor H.Craig Heller

When you cannot sleep (insomnia):

Following the suggestions below can pretty much assure a good night's sleep. Don't force yourself to sleep. it is a natural human activity and it should be a joy to dive into a comfortable bed and sleep. Following are many suggestions that may help you, they all really come under the category of Cognitive Behavioral Therapy.

It is you, living consciously about your own sleep practices and correcting those that are not helpful or even become obstacles to a good night sleep and healthy living, which will allow your well rested body and mind to work full speed ahead to help you loose those extra pounds!

What to do if you don't fall asleep right away:

1. Breathe.

2. Progressive muscle relaxation.

3. Meditation: body scan, one point focus and using a mantra are all good and easy to do. Counting sheep also works! Just counting works.

4. Get up for a short time. Stretch for a minute. Look at a magazine, but stay away from Google or you'll be up all night! Don't eat. Don't drink more than a few swallows of water.

5. Seek Cognitive Behavioral Therapy. You can find specialists in your area at the website of American Academy of Sleep Medicine. **www.sleepeducation**.

Every time, I vote for meditation. It is safest, least expensive and comes in a variety of ways. Refer to the various ways to meditate in this workbook or find a meditation center near you.

Medications and more: Sleep medications can interfere with and even change our circadian clock and according to Dr Heller's research can cause addiction to those drugs, at the same time that we are trying to release our addiction to food!

If you have tried all the natural things suggested here and want to take drugs please make sure to consult your physician.

Sleep aids in one form or another are big business. In 2015 the global market for sleep aids, which encompasses everything from therapeutic pillows (silk eye masks) to sleeping pills was estimated at $62 billion, according to P & S Market Research. Expectations include growth of 6.3% through 2022.

Questions: Assuming you may still have some problems with sleep, please review the items mentioned in this lesson that can help and be honest with which ones you have tried, note the results and which ones you are willing to try now. Maybe you sleep well but still want to change some of the habits mentioned here.

What is still preventing me from getting 7-9 hrs of uninterrupted sleep?

Practices

If you are not satisfied with the amount and quality of sleep you are getting, please answer this question for yourself: Am willing to try these methods to help me sleep?

Choose from the many suggestions in
Lesson 3, Lesson 16, lesson 22 and here in lesson 45

_____   _____

_____   _____

_____   _____

Off to bed now before the next cycle comes or
you are up another 4 hours

Week-end 9

Comments below from James Mackenzie written in Dr Bieler's book, *"Food is your best Medicine"* pages 126-128. Sir James MacKenzie was a British doctor from London who gave up his city practice, returning to his small home town in Scotland to take up the practice of preventative medicine. These are his quotes.

In answering the question what bad habits lead to disease? He says:

1. *Diseases are the result of long developing processes which often begin early in life and finally lead to **saturation of the body with toxins.***

2. *Improper eating, living and thinking habits are the prime cause of this degeneration and toxic saturation.*

3. *The same type of toxin when localized in a joint causes arthritis; when localized in the liver hepatitis, in the kidneys nephritis, in the skin dermatitis, in the pancreas, diabetes and in the the brain, insanity.*

On Changing Habits:

Old habits I am discarding

1.
2.
3.

New habits I am taking on:

1.
2.
3.

Comments about habits I have been working on:

Practices:

45 minutes walking!!!
Sleeping like a baby by now?
How small a plate can you get your dinner onto?
Focus on healthy foods and stay away from ice cream!

Lesson 46: Managing Stress

Laughter is the best medicine

In lesson 25 we talked about why we get stressed, in lesson 41 about how we can be supported. Here we are looking at some ways to go into action to de-stress our lives. Today we note sleep, music, food and laughter as action plans to help us.

Sleep:

You know already that good sleep will help manage your life and your reactions to stress. Not having enough sleep can actually be the cause of your stress. During these 12 weeks, you are being asked to change habits and think differently. That is stressful itself. You need the 7-9 hours of sleep every night. Lights out at same time. If you need a nap to rest the mind and emotions during the day, find a quiet place and relax yourself for a nap. The vicious cycle of inadequate sleep causes the brain and body to get out of whack and only gets worse with time. Turn the TV off earlier and remove it from your bedroom. Use the record button to make a copy of something you think you will miss.

Sound/Music

Allow music to break the tension in your emotional/mental reactions whether in preparing for sleep or just for a few minutes during the day. Driving off the road to a parking area and listening to a cd in your car or music from your phone can be just what you need to change the emotional quotient. Even 5-10 minutes will be a big help.

Playing calm music has a positive effect on the brain and body. It can lower blood pressure and reduce cortisol, a hormone linked to stress.

Some comments about food and stress:

- Stress levels and a proper diet are closely related.
- When we have the most stress we forget to eat well, instead resort to sugary, fatty snack foods as a pick-me up.
- Plan ahead to have dried fruits and nuts in your car for that quick pick me up.
- Less food in your body will make you feel better.
- Fruits and veggies are always good, as is fish with high levels of Omega-3 fatty acids, which have been known to reduce symptoms of stress
- Caffeine increases blood pressure and causes your hypothalamic-pituitary adrenal axis to go into overdrive. In other words caffeine stresses you out.
- Stay away from sugar (I know..heard that before)
- Drink plenty of water to avoid dehydration.

Laughter

- Laughter releases endorphins that improve mood and decrease levels of the stress causing hormones cortisol and adrenaline.
- Laughter tricks our nervous system into making us happy.
- Laugh at yourself in a mirror, use preplanned imagery, plan a laugh-a-thon with a friend.

One of my favorite poems is by Ella Wheeler Wilcox called "Solitude". I share a few lines:

Laugh and the world laughs with you:
Weep and you weep alone.
For the sad old earth must borrow its mirth...
.... Feast and your halls are crowded;

It can also be you who helps another let loose of their hold on stress.

Don't take yourself too seriously

Live in the moment and the stress will subside.
Hold dear the good from the past,
and let go of the rest.
Envision the best for the future,
but let go of the outcome.
Gently teach yourself the art of living now
Now is all you have.

WEEK 10

Lesson 47: Dealing with a bad hair day

"If you are willing to look at another person's behavior toward you as a reflection of the state of their relationship with themselves rather than a statement about your value as a person, then you will, over a period of time, cease to react at all.
Yogi Bhajan SOM 9/6/17

Saying to yourself "they are having a bad hair day" is one easy way to get your mind centered regarding someone else's behavior toward you. Sometimes words and actions you experience create negative thoughts and feelings. You turn to self condemnation and through all kinds of twists and turns eventually come back to eating!

In an ideal world we would all listen to each other, be compassionate and kind. We would never say things that sounded like judgements about us or our family. Sometimes we or they are just being honest and expressing fears or concerns. The problem arises when we take personally what has been said, written or implied.

The prolific writer, Don Miguel Ruiz, in his book, "*The Four Agreements*" addresses this issue in the second agreement. The second agreement is: Don't take anything personally. The first is: Be impeccable with your word. The third is: Don't make assumptions. And the last is: Do your best.

He tells us that we take it personally because we believe that it is true. Let's say you just returned from an interview for a job. It looks good. You are being asked to come back for a second interview. You tell a friend. She laughs and says "You don't want to work at your age! There are lots of younger people out there looking. The competition is huge. Do you really think you'll get the job?" What happens to you next depends upon the ability you have to not take it personally. First it was your interview and you have a vision of doing that job and know you not only can do it but you'd do it better than anyone you know or can imagine. You have the skills and the desire.

You are faced with several internal responses. You could say to yourself. Well, do I really want to work full time? Maybe it's time for me to have time off for the next 20 years. Then the negative side continues until at last you are convinced that your friend is right. Some 30 year old will get that job, so you should prepare to be turned down and forget about the job.

Or, you could say "My friend is having a bad hair day!" SHE doesn't want to work, SHE is afraid of competition. SHE likes the non-structure of her current life and doesn't want to change. So her response to me is really all about her. When you have been able to see that, you will understand what she is saying and know what you are envisioning and walking toward is good for you. You will recognize that she might not have been the best person with whom to share your hopes and excitement.

When you take things personally you often feel offended and tend to get on the defensive, like you have to make yourself right. It is a question of discernment about what someone else has said and many times there is not enough time for a response. That means often the best response is no response. You log into your mind and see your friend's response to what you meant to be good news is not understood the way you meant it. You let it go. The subject gets changed. And months later you invite her to lunch to celebrate your new job.

There are of course many other scenarios. Some include off hand remarks about you when you are the one having a bad hair day. Or when you are discouraged about something, say a relationship that is floundering. The opinions they give you are related to their truths not yours. I have been very blessed in my life to have a friend who always listened, asked more questions and I knew that she cared about my feelings. She didn't try to judge, change my feelings or make me wrong. She just reassured me that she heard my heart.

Don Miguel Ruis says: "Taking nothing personally helps you to break many habits and routines that trap you in the dream of hell and cause needless suffering….."

When you make it a strong habit not to take anything personally, you avoid many upsets in your life. Your anger, jealousy and envy will disappear, and even your sadness will simply disappear if you do not take things personally.

If you can make this second agreement a habit, you will find that nothing can put you back into hell.

What other people do or say to you comes from the agreements they have with themselves, with their world view, not yours. Other people often have wisdom to share. However our personal world is not exactly the same as anyone else's. You must follow your own truth and do what you know is right. In that is freedom and joy.

Write in your journal about some things others have said that you took personally. Also take precaution about what you say to others. Listen and be that friend who cares what they are feeling.

You are only responsible for your own actions.
You are not responsible for the actions of other people.

Lesson 48: Fitness at home

Keeping fit at home. Take a tour around your own home to become aware of new ideas to keep fit right there. Ideas are everywhere; in your kitchen, in cleaning your house, gardening and keeping your home safe, creating a fitness room and doing small hardly noticeable stretching anywhere you are.

"Let's Go, Let's Go" The lady at the gym

In your kitchen

I the morning I do stretches in the kitchen then Qigong in the Meditation room and gentle yoga later in the day. But honestly most of my stretching is spontaneously in the kitchen. I do it while I wait for food to cook or a smoothie to be made, for the microwave to heat up something.

My favorite is the **Big AM Stretch.** Many mornings I use a blender to make a green drink of leafy greens, juice and a banana with or without ice cubes. I have to admit this is amusing for me. I now live in a kitchen with mirrors everywhere so I can see me doing this. I load up the blender and hit Pulse and hold for 10 seconds. This breaks up the ice cubes somewhat. That button needs to be held down or it will shut off.

Then I go to the "Grate" button and am hands free for the rest of making the drink. While it is on "Grate" I lift both arms above my head and count to ten as I alternate each arm reaching higher. I am lifting each one 10 times, up on the right, up on the left, back and forth.

Then I push "Blend" and do the same thing with my arms stretched out as far as I can to each side. I move to the right and to the left 10 times.

Then I push "Shred" which initiates an automatic curving of my right arm over my head like I am doing ballet, as I count to 10 pushing my right arm over head and back in short movements. Next I press "Grind" and do the same with my left hand over my head pushing to the right, 10 times.

The next button is "liquify" (this is on an Oster Blender) and I put both arms behind my head and clasp my fingers together as I bend backwards. The hands are there to protect my head from going too far back, but I get a good shoulder and neck muscle stretch.

Last round is down to the ground. Press the 'Ice Crush" button which on my blender stays running, so I can move. The trick here is to stand up starting with your legs slightly apart for good balance, then take your right arm over your stomach and your left arm to the center of your back, then bend your waist down from the hips. THEN let your arms come down to the floor. Legs can be slightly bent at the knee. If hands don't hit the floor, it is ok, that is what we are working for on this last stretch. You count to ten again, as you gently push down, then back up and down again, a bit more each time.

Most people who are not into fitness and overweight and over 50 just say they can't touch the ground but the trick is to bend down from the waist first. This is easy for me now but it wasn't in the beginning!! I do the whole thing every single day and it has really increasing the ability of my muscles to stretch. Don't do any of this to the point that you feel pain. But a little uncomfortable stretch is ok to feel. This exercise provides an easier way to see progress than most. Nothing special needed.

So you don't make smoothies. Do you use a microwave? and heat up things for 1 minute.? I've just used a lot of this page to describe it, but it takes about 1 minute to do the whole routine. I learned this at the University of Minnesota at age 19 in 1962 when I took modern dance classes!! There is more stretching you can do on the floor but this part is easy and fun…. and works! You can do it at work or visiting friends or by the car if you are driving a long distance and need to get out and stretch. Please try it now. Try it for a week and note your progress.

Cleaning

Instead of going to the gym (or in addition) set a weekly time to vacuum and dust and mop. If you have a cleaning person, cut down to once a month and save the money to buy your new wardrobe and you do the work. Cleaning a house is hard work and uses most of your muscles. How often do you see people in the house cleaning profession that are overweight?

Get a ladder and get up to clean out those closet shelves. Ok a short ladder, a step stool. You may find, up high out of sight, clothing you saved to get into when you lost weight and they have been there for 35 years! Some of the things will be out of style or just something that looked good on you at 20 or 30 but at 50 or 60 just doesn't work. As you lose your weight and try on some of those old clothes, you will wonder why you saved them….Off to the thrift store! I found an old pair of pants that are really not in style now, but I had carefully saved them. I can wear them now and repaired the place they were torn by trying to wear years ago when they got too tight. I am overjoyed that I got up on that ladder to get them and they are walking out to play on me now.

Every day there are little things, bending down, using your muscles to scrub. Things that you didn't do because they were too hard or you got winded. At home you can just stop to rest and do the yoga "corpse" pose (see lesson 58) for 2 minutes and then you are up ready to go again. The result is a cleaner house and some inspiration to keep changing habits and getting more healthy.

Keep your body moving. Rest and move again.
Don't just sit around. Do stretches during the TV commercials.

Gardening: Fitness as you grow your own food.

In the July/August 2010 AARP Magazine a great little article appeared about how we can exercise without belonging to a fitness gym. They suggested exercises that can protect your lower back and knees during the gardening season. A knee pad helps, the knees as well as the Big AM Stretch and loosing weight. What do "they" say? A friend's physician told her "for every pound you are overweight you push 5 more pounds of weight onto your knees". Don't go for the knee surgery before you lose weight and eat right to let those cells repair you.

If you grow veggies and flowers year round in pots you could use this exercise most all year. Did you know that you can burn 300 calories an hour by gardening for one hour. You can also boost bone density and reduce stress.

If you are out **raking** you are using the muscles in your core, shoulders and arms.

The right way to do it is to use short, quick motions and keep the rake close to your body, switch sides every 2-3 minutes.

Pushing a wheel barrow is another way to exercise at home. The muscles used are core, quadriceps, hamstrings, chest, shoulders, arms. The right way to do it is to load the wheelbarrow with only as much weight as you can handle without straining. First use your leg muscles(not your back) to lift the wheelbarrow, next use your arm muscles to push the load forward.

Try getting a medium size pot and potting soil to plant seeds or small new plants. If you got a new pot every week or one big pot each month, in three months you could have yourself a wonderful garden just outside the door.

Plant everywhere, inside, in a garden, on the patio. Plant in the front. One time I envisioned a home with pots on graduating steps and landings leading up to the front door. I was fortunate enough to be able realize that one place I lived. I actually rented only a room but had nearly exclusive use of a nice size patio with steps up to the door and down to another level of patio before it had more steps to the driveway. Pots and pots and pots later, I had a great garden of herbs. It was bordered with pots of luscious zucchini, chard, lettuce, peppers mixed in with my favorite flowers. You could create such a scene to remind you and everyone who visits you, that eating right can be a feast for the eyes as well as the waist line.

It takes bending to cull the plants and add nutrients. It takes effort to get the water to the plants and to harvest and replant if they are seasonal. The patio I am mentioning produced much but was not really in a big space. I went out every morning to water and care for the plants and talk to them.

Here in Arizona we go through the rainy season and even if you live in a planned community, the water and wind can make a mess of your yard and including the public sidewalk. Make sure you are out after a storm with a good outdoor broom containing the debris that can be dangerous to those walking in front of your house. You are getting exercise and being kind to your neighbors and dog walkers. You are taking care of your house and your neighborhood, like you are taking care of you.

A fitness room?

Lucky you if you have a fitness room. One home I lived in had an unused room that I called the yoga room. I used it for meditation, had meditation classes there and also did workouts and danced. There were no machines. It is the scene of the poem I wrote in Lesson 58. It had art work on the walls and cushions that's all except for a fountain for relaxation. The room had one wall open, no doors and was situated near the entrance. Look around your house to find a place that could work, maybe shared usage.

If you live somewhere where there is a basement or you have part of a garage, that also could be a great space to install a treadmill or pilates workout machines. I have a friend who found three huge mirrors in nice frames on craigslist. They were give aways as they were just too big for people to even transport. She got a handyman and his truck to bring them to her basement and hung drapes along the walls to make an elegant workout room…right there at home. Be creative about finding places you can designate as your home fitness center.

References:

AARP Magazine July/August 2010 pages 13 and 14

Dance warm-up exercises from a dance class at the University of Minnesota in 1962.

Donna's fitness room.

Stretches passed on by friends along the way.

WEEK 10

Lesson 49: Got Milk?

Do you love milk? Don't drink it at all? If it is not part of your diet, this lesson will be easier for you. I actually am not in the habit of drinking milk on a daily basis. I keep a small 12 oz bottle of regular milk in the refrig for guests or for a bit in the eggs for scrambled eggs or 1/4 cup on cereal. I even changed to non-fat milk which I used to call 'blue milk' and found it wan't so bad. But I do love yogurt, which I had nearly daily with fresh fruit. Butter, that delicious Irish butter, despite its high calorie content was a favorite. I learned late to drink kefir but oh that Blueberry kefir with all the calories is so delicious and supposed to really help the digestive juices work. I eat cottage cheese and rarely sour cream. We don't need to mention ice cream do we? That is not in my house anymore.

Dairy products like these have lots of good essential nutrients including: calcium, phosphorus, protein, vitamins A, D and B12, riboflavin and niacin. Sometimes cream cheese, cream and butter are not considered "dairy" as they have little calcium.

The common google wisdom lists one of the five food groups to have for a balanced diet as milk and dairy products. This grouping is now the norm instead of a pyramid of foods.

The other four areas are: Carbs, Protein, Fruit/Veggies and Fats/Sugars.

Well, Google isn't the only reporter of milk as a necessary for a balanced diet. Dr Thompson in **"Every Woman's Health"** says it is "an essential food containing a good balance of fats, carbohydrates and proteins as well as a major source of essential minerals and vitamins A and B-2." She explains that "practically all processed milk is enriched with vitamin D." The suggestion from her is that an adult woman should drink 2 cups of milk every day.

Reader's Digest produced a book in 2007 called **"Magic Foods"** in which they stated "Don't Fall for it" Almost everyone has seen the commercials advertising dairy foods as an aid for loosing weight. The trouble is, the results of studies on dairy and weight loss have been inconsistent, with latest showing that people who eat a lot of calcium-rich dairy foods don't in fact have an easier time loosing weight. There is no harm in getting more fat-free milk into your diet; just don't bank on dairy foods to solve your poundage problems." Well, we know it isn't just one kind of food, don't we? It's our habits of eating that solve our poundage problems.

Just to give both sides "The Magic Foods" book, as well as many more advocate milk. They say "to choose fat-free milk (which has more calcium than whole milk) over whole or even 2 per cent which still has a fair amount of saturated fat, the kind that increases the insulin resistance and clogs the arteries."

I just mentioned both sides. So what is the "other" side to dairy? Apparently we lead the world in consumption of dairy products. We are also leading in obesity. The Diamonds, who wrote *Fit for Life* and still run a very successful business, have a different turn on dairy products. You may have a dubious response to the bullet points I will add here for you to consider. First we are told from infancy to drink our milk and that it is good for us. Secondly, some have disqualified the opinions in *Fit for Life* as not scientifically researched well enough. If they were to be accepted by all the major authorities, previously written advice would be wrong and the dairy industry could suffer major loss.

The truth is, in the last 100 years all the major assumptions of science (Newton, Einstein) have been challenged and some we found no longer "true" and we now have a different set of what makes up the universe and what the "laws" of nature are. I was surprised, to say the least, at what I read in *Fit for Life* but it made sense to me.

Here are some of their comments and suggestions. Take a look and if you want to go "no dairy" for a while to check out your own body, do so. That's what this 12 weeks is about, increasing your knowledge and applying it to you to create a healthy you. There are many lactose-intolerant people who do not consume dairy products and are quite healthy.

- According to the LA times in the late 1980's, the American dairy industry is subsidized at about 3 billion dollars a year ($342,000 every hour by tax payers money), that much of it is surplus and sits in storage rotting. The report in the LA Times points out that health benefits of dairy products are commercially motivated. This isn't what the industry says it's what the reporters discovered. Hard to believe that the dairy industry is not paying well to "protect" itself against decline.

- The Diamonds(authors of *Fit for Life*) ask, "cows don't drink cow's milk, so why to humans? No animals drink milk once they are weaned."

- The enzymes necessary to break down and digest milk are renin and lactase and are gone in most humans by the age of three.

- All milk has Casein in it. There is 300 times more Casein in cow's milk than human milk. Casein is for the development of large bones…like cows have. It coagulates in the stomach and forms large tough, dense, difficult-to-digest curds that are adapted for the four-stomach digestive system of a cow. Much energy is needed to rid the human body of this mass of Casein goo that adheres to the lining of the intestines and prevents the absorption of nutrients into the body. Casein is the base of one of the strongest glues in woodworking. Dr. Norman Walker, a health specialist, states that a major contributing factor to thyroid problems is casein.

- Weight loss is 2 or 3 times more difficult if the system is overladen with mucus. The consumption of diary coats the mucus membranes and forces everything to slow down. Vital energy is lost. When a person makes a guttural sound like they are trying to release mucus, they suggest that in many cases the person has been consuming dairy. Actually this is what first caught my attention as both my parents used to do this and I was starting do it too.

- Interviews and their own research brought the Diamonds to the belief that milk and milk products are a major factor in obesity. They learned of tests showing that adults who use dairy do not absorb nutrients as well as others. Poor absorption leads to chronic fatigue.

- We know that there are many places other than dairy where we can find an abundance of calcium. Proponents of dairy fail to mention the other places to find calcium. The Diamonds state that "raw sesame seeds contain more calcium than any other food on earth." They also point out that most fruit contains "ample" calcium. The best sources of calcium are Sesame seeds, all raw nuts(1/2 c a day is plenty), kelp, all leafy greens, and concentrated fruits such as figs, dates and prunes.

- *Fit for Life* mentions that cutting back on dairy can cause peeling or brittle nails or hair loss. They suggest increasing the better kind of calcium in the items mentioned above. As you replace the calcium in milk with other sources, so will your body replace the damaged nails/hair with healthier hair and nails.

With the controversy that followed the sale of over 12 Million *Fit For Life* books back in the 1980's, it is to be noted that authors of *Fit to Life* state (on page 113) "To prevent yourself from throwing your hands up in disgust or frustration, make your own decision based on your resources." It's up to you. It is you body, your life. It is a big change, unless you are lactose intolerant and already to not consume dairy, but one you might want to try.

Changing habits is, most of the time, not easy. It seems easier to just keep on truckin' doing what you know best. But that got you overweight and you don't want to stay there or you wouldn't be reading this.

If you do decide to try a non-dairy life, I suggest you give it at least a few weeks for your body to get used to, a month or two is better. You then can find calcium substitutes and let your body heal and make new what it can. See Appendix for Some Dairy Definitions

Our bodies are amazing ..... they can heal themselves if we cooperate!

References;

Content of dairy product information from

From. <u>Dairy Nutrition Facts - Midwest Dairy</u>

https://www.midwestdairy.com/nutrition-and-health/dairy-nutrition/

Diamond, Harvey and Marilyn, *Fit For Life,* Warner books 1985,87 p. 104 - 113

Reader's Digest. *Magic Foods* 2007, reader's Digest Association

D.S. Thompson, MD consulting editor, *Everywoman's Health: the complete guide to body and Mind by 15 women doctors.* 20000. Prentice Hall, 1980,1985

WEEK 10

Lesson 50: Digestion

"Digestion: first line of defense against disease".
Dr Bieler

Bieler refers to the digestive system as a chemical refinery manufacturing fuels and delivering energy from the raw materials it is given: proteins, fats, and carbohydrates, which are broken down into starches and sugars, vitamins and minerals. This process takes place in a 30 foot long hollow tube called the alimentary canal. It is really mind boggling to imagine a 30 ft. long tube coiled inside us. No wonder we feel uncomfortable, as it is filled! He likens the canal to an assembly line or conveyor belt with stations where microscopic chemists convert foodstuffs for our body's use by breaking down, diluting and dissolving as well as adding some chemicals and removing others. Busy little chemists at work in our bodies!

Here I add brief points Dr. Bieler makes about the digestive system:

- When food ferments or putrefies in the small intestine, the lining is irritated and its efforts to stop the irritation result in diarrhea or constipation.

- Inflammation occurs with repeated absorption of harmful elements.

- Millions of villi enlarge the surface of the small intestine. At the time that the blood in the villi becomes over charged with toxic elements, harmful materials enter the main blood stream.

- Quantity of food matters. Up to 40 % of the average American diet is rich, fatty, difficult to digest food. The villi in the small intestine have no way to regulate how much to absorb …. when it is too much, a person either becomes ill or obese.

- Quality of food matters. Eating one kind of food at a time eases digestion. "Throughout history the mono-diet was practiced with good results." Bieler.

- Fats, minerals, vitamins and carbohydrates are of vital importance to life. Unneeded fats are sent to various parts of the body to be stored….stored!!! "A physiological fact which saddens and worries overweight Americans. Ah yes…

- "Drug manufacturers and advertisers seem to be obsessed with the digestive system. Pharmacy shelves are lined with a fantastic array of patent medicines, pills and food supplements for digestive malfunctions. Americans squander millions on these products. If they knew something of body chemistry, they would realize they could use "dietary medicine" instead of pills to cure their digestive disorders."

"You can't ignore the importance of a good digestion. The joy of life depends on a strong stomach, whereas a bad digestion inclines one to skepticism, incredulity, breeds black fancies and thoughts of death."
Quote from Joseph Conrad

It is said that poor digestion can incline you to depression.

Certain types of yogurt contain probiotic bacteria that can improve the function of your intestine. Having a healthy intestine may help protect against inflammation and leptin resistance, which is one of the main hormonal drivers of obesity. Make sure to choose yogurt with live, active cultures, as other types of yogurt contain virtually no probiotics.

Also, consider choosing full-fat yogurt. Studies show that full-fat dairy — but not low-fat is associated with a reduced risk of obesity and type 2 diabetes over time. Low-fat yogurt is usually loaded with sugar, so it's best to avoid it.

Summary Probiotic yogurt can increase your digestive health. Consider adding it to your weight loss diet but make sure to avoid products that contain added sugar

Dr Beiler quotes below referring to his patients.

"When their bodies are freed of the toxic load they carry, an almost magical change takes place in the patients I have treated."

Suggestions:

- Eat simple meals without many different foods
- If you are cleaning your intestines, eat non-spicy foods, vegetables raw or lightly cooked, fruit, but eaten separately.
- Eat less, eat slowly.
- Eat like a Hobbit, small amounts more often.

References

Dr Henery G Bieler,MD. *Food is your Best Medicine. Pages 54-61*

Week 10 Week-end

Go back and look at lesson 15. Read it through and read your story then

Today you see a skinny, beautiful, energy filled person!!

Imagine the perfect you. Draw a picture, find a photo of you not fat, write or sketch a portrait of what you look like, how you move, what you are doing with your life, who lives with you in that picture? Attach here or on the other side. This really isn't "homework", just have fun with it, if you want to.

On Changing Habits:

Old habits I am discarding

1.
2.
3.

New habits I am taking on:

1.
2.
3.

Comments about habits I have been working on:

Practices:

50 minutes of walking!
Got milk? Or trying to do without dairy?
Been busy stretching at home?
Don't take anything personally. Smile.

Lesson 51: Life Commandments

You can begin a new pattern. You can tell a new story.

What are Life Commandments?

Life Commandments are deep internal belief systems that act as the guidance gyros of your mind. They are a chronic pattern thought. You can begin a new pattern. You can tell a new story. Your internal belief systems were originally there to help you, at least someone thought they would help you. They set patterns for acceptable behavior. They have been a part of us for so long that we are not aware of them. We just obey them intuitively. We keep adding new ones. They affect out speech and our behavior.

Our deep internal belief systems ultimately affect all of our belief systems, about religion and education and relationships as well as about our bodies. They inform why and what we believe about our world and about ourselves? We received them from authority figures early in our lives. How do they affect our behavior? It is possible to change a belief that has become dysfunctional or sick.

People usually break early commandments between the ages of 17-25. Can you think of any? drinking? driving a car? having friends of different ages? calling adults by their first names instead of Mr and Ms? There are appropriate times to obey and appropriate times to break these life commandments. As an adult some commandments need to be broken and are not. An example is holding a parents hand when crossing the street at age 2-3, which becomes unnecessary at age 15. Accepting a new inner belief system is similar to acquiring a new habit. You have to get rid of the past thinking and replace it with something new. Times when you break a commandment may produce guilt. Some examples are; I can't eat dessert first. I should accept what people offer me and eat it. Not doing so is impolite and disrespectful.

We need helpful life commandments that match our life now.

The function of our own seeking self understanding and maturity is to help us break the life commandments that keep us from growing mentally, physically, emotionally and spiritually to be healthy. Life commandments run the gamut of our vast mixture of experience. It is our focus here to look at the habits that disallow or make difficult our ability to live integrated lives, especially in the area of weight and self care.

Here is a story from "Listening & Caring Skills" by Dr. John Savage that might sound familiar. *"Since I was born during the depression, I have become aware of a whole series of life commandments from that era. One of those very hard to break even from this day is "eat everything on your plate". Think of all those little boys and girls who will starve to death in China if you don't eat it all!"*

I often wondered how the food on my plate was going to get to China, at least without getting moldy. Other cultures have the same problem. Several years ago in the New Yorker Magazine, I saw a cartoon of a Chinese mother saying "Now children, be sure to eat all your rice, because in America children have only junk food."

Once beliefs are anchored in our minds by reward, the belief becomes internalized and we accept it as truth. The truths support our understanding of the world and who we are. Did you hear things like: "fat people are ugly" or stupid or bad? Or "no wonder people don't like Susie, look at how fat she is". "Never tell what goes on in this family. That is airing our dirty laundry!" And we kept the secrets and never had any help because no one knew. Mother says "you will never find a boy friend because you are too fat!" Or "your ears are too big, you should hide your ears."

Often we accept these Life Commandments and keep believing them as if they were eternal truth. But the eternal truth is you have the power within you to change them.

You just have to find them first. Please take some time now to begin to note your life commandments that have prevented you from thinking and acting in a mature way about food and about your body.

1. What are some early beliefs like "clean plate club" or eat now, we may not have enough tomorrow?

2. What are some verbal commandments? (To be polite you must eat what people serve you)

3. What are some life commandments you believed by inference? This is the most difficult. You inferred that someone meant something by what they said but never checked it out. You meet an old neighbor and talk about getting together. This is repeated and she never calls. You feel rejected. Then one day you see her at a restaurant. She comments on how great you look and wants to set a time to have lunch. There go the assumptions! What beliefs can you identify that are based on assumptions?

4. What life commandments about your well-being are related to behavior you have observed?

Let's let other people form this life commandment from us "If I change my habits and make a commitment to healthy new ones, I too can lose all of my excess weight!!!

Be willing to be disobedient to the negative life commandment

WEEK 11

Lesson 52: Sweets and eating out

There are things in life that are some times just not easy. Dealing with sweets and eating out are two of them. Most of us do not want to commit to never eating sweets again or never going out to eat. We don't have to. What you choose to do will be easier if you think about it ahead. So let's do some thinking and problem solving.

Eating out may involve a variety of situations. Here are some of them with suggestions that will help us enjoy our time and not come home feeling, stuffed, guilty, disappointed in ourselves, depressed or like a failure. Remember we are changing habits so consider these scenarios.

A potluck (or a buffet) is the most dangerous because there is a temptation to try some of everything and your digestive system will not like having so many different kinds of food, or so much. So wander by the food first to see what there is. Avoid foods that have too many ingredients and you don't know what is in them. Avoid foods with sugar. Then pick out 2-3 things that look good, like salad(s), veggies, fish or other protein foods. If you are tempted by desserts, wait until you have eaten the main foods first. You may have eaten enough and decide you don't need the sweets after all.

A cocktail party may only last a while and you may be able to eat before or after. In that case, taste something and spend your time listening and sharing with people. That's what it is really about..not the food. If it is your dinner, then pick the healthiest thing you can see and take 1 or 2 pieces. Then go back for one more or again another time for another piece. Avoid making a big plate and eating it all right away. Regarding drinking; you can add ice to a class of wine, you can ask for water and let them think you are drinking vodka and water, if that matters to you. You can ask for sparkling water or iced tea. It is easy to tally up many calories drinking alcohol at a party when you are just standing around. Get your drink and go back for water, if you need to hold onto something.

A big special dinner like wedding, graduation, birthday, or other celebrations. You can usually have a choice of items but if not just leave on your plate what you don't want. That is better than eating something you really don't like. Enjoy the people, the music, the place and listen and tell stories and you will have less time to eat and have much more fun.

A lunch or dinner with a small group of friends, business associates or clients. Here you will be able to order what you want. You may be able to share a dinner or save part of it to take home, allowing you to indulge in minimalist eating!

A meal at someone else's home If they ask what you can eat, tell them you are watching your weight and health and you love such and such and don't eat sugar or starches or whatever is on your "avoid list". You may be surprised how much people often go out of the way to accommodate you when you say you are working on being healthy. If they don't ask, then just eat what you know is good for you and leave the rest. You do not need to "make them feel good" by eating beyond your comfort zone.

A dinner party or luncheon at your home Make your menu to include items that you will want to eat yourself if left over. If they are meat eaters and you are not, buy enough meat just for them. Send them home with the dessert.

Out for a roof top happy hour split an appetizer or get one that is ok for you. Order the drink that fits your "program". You are there to visit with friends.

A romantic dinner for two split something, avoid the extras or some of them like starters and soup and bread and dessert. Eye gaze in place of eating.

Food at a restaurant the kids love where they can run around and play. This can be difficult because many of these places have fast food menus. Check out the menu offered ahead of time. Bring a bag of trail mix if you need to, but most of those places will include a small salad. Just stay away from the fried stuff.

A quick stop meal on the road stop for drinks but bring your own food.

You forgot to eat a meal, you are out and need food: bring items you can leave in your glove compartment for a low calorie pick me up or stop at the grocery store for a small bottle of juice, trail mix or piece of fruit.

Sweets

You are probably not going to turn into a frog, gain 20 lbs or ruin your body if you occasionally have an ice cream cone, a dessert, chocolate or some other sugar laden item. Well, you could avoid donuts at any cost.

What we are doing here is making new habits so during this time while you are losing the actual weight off your body, just stop eating sugar. If you do this for a number of months, sugar will never taste the same. You will take a bite of an apple pie and notice how sickeningly sweet most of them are, same with donuts.

If you want to partake of a birthday desert, a spoonful will make the point that you stand together in celebration. Try starting to say "I don't eat sugar". If you think you will be tempted re-read lesson 38.

If you fall off the wagon. Breathe and get back on. But don't waste any energy with self deprecation. Just smile and say to yourself. Next time…it will be easier. The fact that you are mindful of what you are doing makes a difference. It will be easier next time.

Enjoy social situations for the beautiful souls that meet together,
not for the food consumed.

WEEK 11

Lesson 53: A stroll through the grocery store

This is a "Field Trip"! If you can't do this today, try to do it over the week-end. Why? Because you will learn a lot about prices, ingredients, calories and good buys as well as best times to shop and what to buy where. It will help you make better choices about maintaining a healthy body.

Preparation:

- This is a little work, so I recommend you take a friend and compare notes.
- Pick a grocery store where they have a cafe in the store, so you can stop if you are tired or want to add notes at the end of the "shopping" time.
- Make up your grocery list of the items you need in the next week. You need not buy them if you do not need food, but take the list.

At the store find **fresh veggies and fruits:**

Check prices on 6 foods in the produce area that you usually buy, compare with Organic

	Food item	Regular	Organic
1.			
2.			
3.			
4.			
5.			
6.			

Ask one of the employees in that area when new produce comes in and when is the best day and time of day to shop with least amount of people. If you are being pressured by crowds it can affect your stress level, compelling you to either not get what is on your list at all or settle for what you find most quickly.

Head to the **Dairy area t**o check foods there. Are there specials? and is there an item that in unfamiliar to you? Check out the labels for ingredients, amount of protein and calories. Check out alternates to butter and other dairy products.

My finds in dairy and cheeses:

On to **juices,** first refrigerated, then unrefrigerated in the center aisles. Look at the sugar content, especially if there is added sugar. DO NOT buy juices with added sugar. Those without added sugar already have enough. Many of the tasty sweet juices you find in the non refrigerated aisles are full of sugar.

My finds:

Look for the **Cereal** aisle: Pick 3 or 4 of your favorite cereals. Take your time looking at the content

Name of cereal	price	amt of sugar.	amt of protein.	amt of carbs
1.				
2.				
3.				
4.				

Did you notice that Shredded Wheat is least calories and no sugar?

Do not get discouraged, buy what you need. This exercise is to help you understand, on a very basic level, what you are eating every day, mostly what it is costing you in dollars and nutrition to achieve your own level of well-being.

You might have passed the **frozen foods,** which generally I do not recommend you buy. Stop and check out three brands of Ice Cream and 3 brands of Pizza. For content and price.

Ice Cream Item	*Content*	*Price*
1.		
2.		
3.		

Pizza Item	*Content*	*Price*
1.		
2.		
3.		

Many people who buy fresh organic food have agreed that it is best to pretty much stay out of the middle aisles of the grocery store. But check the items you love the most there to understand what you are really eating. If you find any with high fructose sugar, smile and return them to the shelf.

My middle aisle finds:

Back to **Meat/Poultry and Fish**: Look it all over, check prices. Find a few items in all those categories, if you eat all of them.

Item	*When it came to store?*	*From?*	*Been Frozen?*	*Local?*
1.				
2.				
3.				

If you can get a time to ask questions of the butcher, ask when they came into the store, where they came from and are they already frozen and thawed. In big stores they are mostly pre-frozen because they transport and sell large quantities. So you are probably re-freezing if you can't eat the product in a day or so. Second? Third time frozen? Ask if any of these items are purchased locally? Also ask when new deliveries of fresh items come to the store and if you can order ahead. Sometimes you can.

Bakery Goods: Most of the bakery goods that are baked in chain stores are made ahead and frozen, then put into a baker for 8 to 10 minutes. They come out smelling wonderful and if they are whole grains with other good things they can be delicious if eaten soon. They have preservatives that are best to avoid but actually keep the bread longer than most bread you can buy at a bakery.

Of course, best deal is to make your own bakery items and add all the good things…but we can't all do that or even want to. Nonetheless the "fresh baked" goods from a chain store bakery are better for you than most of the other breads in the long aisle with bread. Again look at the labels here also to check sugars, carbs, protein and calories.

My finds:

Honestly, this is mostly a "check the labels" exercise that none of us usually do because we are in a hurry when we shop. It is also a time to ask questions and learn a lot from the people in charge of each department.

It is worthwhile to do the same thing in markets like Whole Foods, Trader Joes, Sprouts or markets that sell fresher goods. If you live in a place where you can buy eggs from the farmer or go to local farmer's markets that is always preferable. The quality of the food is most always higher and you are supporting your neighbors.

Once you have done this big check up on grocery buying, you will have a log recorded in your brain that will help you in the future to make comparisons and healthier choices

Have fun shopping!

"Why do you spend your money for that which is not bread
and your labor for that which does not satisfy......
listen diligently to me, and eat what is good."
Isaiah 55:2

WEEK 11

Lesson 54: How to reframe

Forward moving actions happen at the speed
that I am able to release the old thought and accept the new thought.

We have addressed self talk, what we say about ourselves. The first step in changing how we talk about ourselves is to recall and recognize what kind of stories we have been telling ourselves about us. What we have said internally comes out sometimes stronger as we tell others our story.

What are three negative themes you have been repeating about yourself? I am….
(fat, unorganized, forgetful, bossy, too loud or too quiet, scattered or?)

1.
2.
3.

What do you want to say now?

If you were interviewing for a job…best in your life, using all your experience, sterling qualities, the best of you, …what are 8 words you would use to describe you that you think are true, you are saying them thinking of you at you potential best?

1.
2
3
4
5

6
7
8

Many times our old images are so strong that we can't get past their emotional impact to function as healthy mature humans. I share with you one way to reframe images of the past that persist in functioning as obstacles.

A Reframing story:

My brother used to be filled with so much anger and especially at my Dad. One day I asked him why he felt so angry. At that time my brother was in his 50's about 5 years after our father had died.

He recounted a story about him and his twin running away from home at age 10. The fact is they ran away to a friends house and didn't let my parents know and came back about 9:30 to 10 way past sunset. My father took them to the amusement room in the basement. My brother recounted that my Dad hit our brother. I guess he didn't hit both of them. He had been angry at my dad about this for over 40 years.

I asked he if wanted to "reframe the scene". He agreed. So I explained that he was still reacting to the emotions of a 10 year old. He was now in his 50's. Because we lived in the same family I was able to reconstruct what was likely to have been the situation. As I spoke I was careful to describe the scene as we might have seen it through adult eyes without emotional words.

I reminded him that Mom and Dad usually had a cocktail before dinner. Their two sons (I was 6 months old at that time) did not come home for dinner. I imagine Mom send Dad out in the car to look for them in the neighborhood. He came home empty handed and they ate and had another drink. Both of my parents came from divorced families, where they had grown up without a father to discipline them. So neither had an example of how they should behave. Back then, in the early 1940's, the common societal belief was that the man was the guy to confer the discipline. I told my brother that I could almost hear my mother saying "You have to discipline them, dear!"

So he took them down to the recreation room and spanked, hit??? But my brother told me my Dad didn't do a knock down fight. It sounded like the boys were surprised. I would have been surprised too because I never saw my Dad hitting anyone.

We got done reframing the childhood scene with grown-up eyes and it looked different.

I think he began to see how hard it might be to be a young couple that had to care for and teach and love not just one first child but twins, who by the way had their own language. My parents had no idea what they were saying to each other. I did notice the general level of anger in my brother subsided after that time of reframing.

What habits are you still carrying around to foster the old images? What feeds it? What can you do to change that?

Please use this method if you'd like to reframe some of the stories in your life that have had negative affects upon you and in the end have contributed to your weight gain or other habits that you now want to change. Go to your journal and jot down what comes to your mind and write about it now or later. It will help.

Sometimes as you lose the old you and find the new you, occasions will arise without formal framing to help you change a self image. I had spent over 15 years looking in stores for large and extra large, size 2X clothes. I walked into a shop to purchase a new blouse for my most recent birthday. The clerk looked over the rack and picked my size and handed it to me as she walked me to the dressing room. I stopped to glance at the size and tears welled up in my eyes, when I saw that she had given me a size small! So now I am a size small and the sales clerk reframed that image for me. I wore it with a pair of pants marked 4-6! I am grateful. Now I just look for size small in the clothing stores!

WEEK 11

Lesson 55: Walking as spiritual encounter, sport and recreation

The world turns different colors as you walk through it.

This week you are walking 55 minutes a day. I hope you have found beauty along the way on your walks these three months. I hope you have also found peace and joy. I found those and many other things as I have observed and reflected along my walks. One day my dog, Obi and I were walking past a group of teens waiting for the bus to school. I saw them quite a bit ahead so I had time to view the scene from the distance. The group of about 10 kids on the corner in front of a group of giant cactus. The cactus were green with some purple but so was the hair on three of the students, both males and females. I was watching how a different generation learns about relationships at young ages. I wrote a poem and share it with you. It is a product of morning walking. Something I would have missed, without kids at home, if I hadn't been out walking.

Purple and Green

They stand firm, some slouched
in the morning sun, waiting
each holding tight to their link to the
world; calling in images, facts, words,
meaning, any meaning to add credence
to an unspoken hope to belong.

Like a modern museum, they
exhibit a vast array of art work
on every possible place
their bodies can display.

Not a word passes between them,
not a glimpse at those who pass by.
They stand as sentinels of an era
waiting to coalesce.

Purple, green and every imaginable
color in between, paints a diverse
picture of heads immersed in the
very serious work of self discovery.
Not a smile in sight for blocks.

Where have all the children gone,
long time passing?

A.M. of May 4th, 2016 watching school children waiting for the bus

When we walk alone, the nature muses come out to talk and teach us about clouds, and big glowing circles around the moon and how water courses its way down hills loosening rocks and making new earthscape. When we walk alone we find that we are not alone as we watch the lizard doing push ups, and the quail bringing the brood out of the bushes to look for breakfast. We see a mother bobcat looking for its run-away cub and point to show her where he went. And when we walk alone we notice the dazzling colors shouting from cactus in bloom and marvel both at the beauty and not finding them the next day. They understand living now and are good teachers. So I recommend walking alone. It is good for the soul.

Walking with friends: I understand why Steve Jobs always wanted to have walking meetings. It takes away the tension of sitting face to face wondering what the other will say and what you will say back. You relax and what you say is less studied and more honest. If you are walking daily alone in the same area and want to have a walking buddy, it doesn't need to be someone who is already a friend. If you see the same person time after time, stop to visit and ask if they'd like to join you once a week or more. It takes overcoming the life commandment that says you shouldn't interact with strangers, if that is a part of you.

I have often seen as many as five people walking together on a daily basis. Of course you block the advantages of walking alone but it does a great deal for relationships and we need to have solid functioning, inspiring relationships to live an integrated balanced life!

Get out there and run: 3 - 5 k Marathons

Sign up for a marathon and you'll be telling yourself you are serious! Yes, I am serious! But don't sign up yet. Do some homework. First check out the walk/run marathons in your area. They are mostly fundraisers for non-profit endeavors. Find one you want to support and what time of year they run. Choose one 6 months to a year ahead, depending on your current ability to walk/run.

Most of them charge about $40 to join and are 1-5 K runs. 5k is just over 3 miles. 3 K is 1.86 miles, so that's easy for you by now. Next step is to start the training. You are already walking every day so this will be "upping the level" for you. I suggest you start to walk at a faster pace, little by little, just like you did with increasing walking time. As you do your daily walk, begin alternating 5 mins of each 30 min walk with very easy fast walking and speed up, arriving at slow, soft runs. Don't pound the pavement. When you are on the actual marathon, you can slow even to a walk and then speed up and no one will care if you just walk the whole thing. Let your body set the speed and slow downs. Let your heart rest if you start running so fast that you can't talk at the same time.

Start up and end the race with warm up stretches like the ones you have learned in this class. If you are connected to a gym or have a treadmill, take one day a week to walk for 30 mins, increasing speed and incline each month. This can be over the whole year. No-one is in a hurry. You will be proud of yourself to finish the marathon and it is a fun event to do with others. You up your health, donate to a charity and have fun doing it

Walking Trips

Yes, there are companies that produce walking trips all over the world. Or you can plan your own. Go to places you have always wanted to go. Plan ahead, so you can get reservations at special locations. For example many people dream of a hike along the Ocean or in the Grand Canyon or in the Tetons or? Whether you are camping, staying at medium priced hotels or going to famous lodges, the places you want to go get booked ahead at the time of year you and everyone else wants to go. Booking ahead also gives you some extra time to get your trekking legs out and in shape. And your looking ahead is also a sweet gift that lifts you up to expectation and joy.

When will you go on a walking trip to celebrate? _____

With whom? _____

You may want to go with a company that plans treks. Most them have guides and some include prepaid meals. I am not recommending these above others. They are just here so you can see what they do. Ask friends, go online and you will find more.

OARS: www.oars.com. They plan hikes, some with river rafting and boating experiences. Their trips span several days to a month including camping or rustic cabins or hotels in cities and are all over the world.

The **Wildland Trekking Company** has more than 9,000 members. Sleeping bags, backpacks etc are included in the price of the trip. Below is a quotation of what they offer. Other companies may offer a similar array. Tell them what you are looking for and what your limitations are and they will help you find a trip, organize it and keep you safe. It takes the stress out of trip planning if that's not your pleasure. Here is the write up of what they offer.

Our tour offerings range from strenuous, off-trail backpacking adventures - to on-trail, moderate hiking and backpacking trips - to inn-based and basecamp hiking vacations. Our destinations range from the Sierra Nevada Mountains in California to the Great Smoky Mountains in North Carolina, with the Desert Southwest and Rockies in between. And our Global Destinations include Peru, Ecuador, Patagonia, Nepal and Iceland. This diversity allows you to enjoy the world's inspiring landscapes in a variety of ways and at different times in your life.

Others are: **backroads.com, theranchmalibu.com,** and **stridetravel.com gives you 192 hiking and walking tours.** It's all there.

Keep walking toward your goal of an integrated, whole you.

Week end 11

On Changing Habits:

Old habits I am discarding

1.
2.
3.

New habits I am taking on:

1.
2.
3.

Comments about habits I have been working on:

Practices:

55 minutes each day…almost to walking goal!!!
Plan a walking trip?
Know your grocery stores.
Pull up anchor on obstructions to your well-being
Are you living what you believe?

Lesson 56: Mindful living as daily practice

Life itself is the real teacher,

and how we meet it moment by moment the real meditation practice.
Jon Kabat Zin from his forward in ***"Mindfulness Based Stress Reduction"***

Is mindfulness a form of meditation?

Yes, it is a form of insight meditation as opposed to concentration. Many of the world's religions use concentration meditation either as an end or a path to merging with God.

In Christianity, Hinduism and in many of the religions, we focus with the goal of merging or becoming one with whatever is our focus. Sometimes that is aided by concentration on a concept, or an image or a mantra. A mantra is a word or phrase that we say repeatedly. In Zen we seek to empty our minds of all, so that we may simply be.

Mindful meditation calls you to notice everything, to become aware. "You begin to discover the causes of your own suffering and find a pathway to greater freedom." (Stahl) It calls you to notice the smells and sounds around you, how your body is feeling, how something tastes or what you hear your mind saying.

It is hot and you have been in meetings all morning and on the way home you know the Yogurt shop is just blocks away. You hear your mind saying "I wonder what their special flavors are today?" You are aware that this is leading to a stop for a frozen yogurt. You smile and say "I hear you!" That sounds nice. "Maybe there is a cold sparkling water bottle in the frig at home."

You slide by the turn to the yogurt shop and are aware that you are aware of your body's reaction to heat and over doing. You are aware that you and the fat-eating cells have made a wise decision. You were being mindful of your goals by not giving in. But you were also acknowledging the situation and able to distance yourself to make a wise choice. You realize it has taken days, weeks, month upon month to lose what you have already lost. You have decided that two minutes of unwise choice is not going to set you back! You notice how satisfied you feel in your decision. The car air conditioner is beginning to cool you off. You sense the tranquility of the moment. All is well. You got to be present during that whole episode. You also have a new image in place to help you next time temptation enters the scene. You have rehearsed your new line in life's ever changing drama.

Bob Stahl and Elisha Goldstein wrote the workbook that is used for the course called **MBSR** or **Mindfulness Based Stress Reduction.** They originated this class to help people who were in pain, whose doctors were unable to find a way to help them.

They give us 8 attitudes essential to mindfulness practice. I have taken this class 2 times and have found their advice to be gold. I am listing these for you and adding that the simple way to embrace mindful living is becoming aware. I mean noticing not judging. Allowing your self to look at nature, your thoughts, what is said or not said.

It is being the person who watches, not the problem solver or the critic. We are well trained to do that by all the people we meet growing up. You are capable of training yourself to think and act differently.

Here are the 8 attitudes of mindfulness from The MBSR workbook.

Beginner's mind: having an open mind with a sense of curiosity

Non-judgement: lack of judgement, impartial observation, not labeling, but taking note of thoughts, feelings, sensations in each moment

Acknowledgement: acceptance of what is

Non-striving: lack of fear, not trying to get anywhere but where you are

Equinimity: living with with a sense of balance which leads to wisdom

Letting be: Letting go of old outcomes, patiently waiting for new ones and rejoicing in what comes to be

Self reliance: confidence in your own experience

Self compassion: loving you as you are, without self blame or criticism

You can purchase this book online or at bookstores. It includes a CD with meditations and yoga stretches, from 3 minutes to 45 mins in length. You can download it to your computer and play it on your phone. If you want to prepare for sleep or calm your anxiety or just take a break and relax, this is a wonderful way to do it.

I hope you will take time with each of these eight attitudes. Think about them. Write in your journal, Relate them to stories of your own life. Being mindful involves a lifestyle change that happens first in what you believe about yourself and reaches out to everything you think and do.

Mindfulness is noticing your life. It is enjoying your breakfast so much that by dinner time you still remember what you had for breakfast.

Be mindful

Be mindful of what you are eating, when, how fast

Be mindful that you are eating what is making a healthy you

Be mindful of the grocery purchases that you do not need to make

Be mindful of how long food sits in your refrigerator

Be mindful of taking care of yourself

Be mindful of loving others, of listening and of caring

Be mindful of keeping your body moving and in good condition

Be mindful of resting your body in sleep allowing your cells to maintain, repair and clear out the extra fat

Be mindful to not take other's behavior personally

Be mindful of old outdated food on your shelves

Be mindful, all the time, of the vision you have of a beautiful, healthy you

Be mindful of the new thoughts you carry about who you are
and allow the old thoughts to dissolve and disappear

Be mindful to avoid conflict and create peace, so you may live without stress

Be mindful to do and say what you believe

Be mindful to smile and live with joy

Be mindful to keep creating the new you and keep helping others to see the best in themselves.

Be mindful so you may be at peace
May all beings be at peace

Suggested reading for mindfulness; These are all wonderful books you may enjoy.

The Dalai Lama (translated by Jeffery Hopkins) ***"How to Practice:*** *the way to a Meaningful Life"*, 2002, Atria Books, New York Read chapter 5. 'Extending help'

Goleman, Daniel, ***Focus, The Hidden Driver of Excellence***, 2013, HarperCollins, New York, NY. Read pages 186-189 Breathing Buddies chapter 17.

Santorelli, Saki, ***Heal Thy Self; Lessons on mindfulness Medicine,*** 1999, Bell Tower, New York. Takes you through a seven week self inquiry in 247 pages..wonderful

Singer, Michael A. *"**The Untethered Soul:** the journey beyond yourself."* 2007, New Harbinger Publications,Inc. P.127-137 Chapter 14 on "Clinging"

Stahl,Bob and Goldstein, Elisha, ***A Mindfulness based Stress Reduction Workbook***, 1998, New Harbinger Publications. Get the CD, take the class.

Thich Nhat Hahn, Essential writings, 2001, Modern Spiritual Masters series Orbis Books, Maryknoll, New York. All excellent. Try p 47 "The eyes of mindfulness"

WEEK 12

Lesson 57: Maintaining

You can't go back to where you where, because it isn't there anymore.
You can only walk on into your new life
with the joy and expectation that you have created.

Sometimes I talk too much. So I leave you here a list of one sentence answers, the explanations of which you know from our work together, in answer to the question "How shall I maintain the work I have done during these 12 weeks?

As we head through this last week, I ask you to stop for a time to consider each of the ways I suggest you can maintain the equanimity, joy, peace and healthy physical status toward which I hope you are by now confidently walking. Each harkens back to one lesson or another, to one quote or story.

This is long enough as it is, so I have made short of the stories, wanting you to add yours as you proceed though these last days of our 3 months. As you move into the future, support yourselves and each other. Do you really need an organization to do this? Find a friend. Make a friend. One or two is good. 10 is ok. Eight is fine and 6 is very fine. If you are doing this alone, connect with your inner you and with others, from time to time. Do not forget to encourage one another on your journey.

How shall I maintain this work begun?

Walking to maintain your stamina, muscles and cells working to keep your body immune

Regular time out daily, weekly, monthly, yearly for vacations and retreats

An attitude of **Mindful living**

Allowing your body to rest and repair in good **sleep** each day

Living in Alignment with your Greater Power and with yourself

Wisely and regularly **consuming the foods** that are best for you, in moderation, and avoiding the foods that break down your body

Continuing to ask yourself the question "How then shall I live"? And **continuing to learn**

Allowing yourself to **re-create yourself,** letting go of habits when they no longer serve you and taking on new ones

Taking seriously your responsibility to **be the example** of healthy living to all people you encounter

Avoiding stress you can not change and allowing your mind to revision each new situation to see the inherent good

Being still and allowing the water to take its course in your life

Celebrating life always

Cynthia+

Lesson 58: Moving on with Yoga and Tai-Chi

As we continue through our last week, I would like to encourage you to seriously entertain the idea of taking up Yoga or Tai Chi, if you are not already doing so. Both are fitness practices that are far beyond just moving your body. Each embraces the concept of an integrated person including fitness, diet and mind/body connections, as well as spiritual awareness that allows you to keep yourself in balance for the rest of your life. Learn about each. Go to lessons at different places and be mindful of your feelings as you are there. Go back to the place that your inner self calls "home."

When we are asking, we find soul mates
to walk, to move, to dance together
on this earth journey.

Yoga

The word yoga means "union" and refers to the belief that one can live in harmony as the body and breath become in a state of union with mind and spirit. It involves controlling the poses of the body to work in coordination with breath.

A Yoga practice involves 5 elements: correct diet, breathing, exercise and relaxation as well as meditation. The body poses are called asanas.

There are places you can learn yoga for free. There are fitness centers to join and sometimes a sports store will give free lessons. Check in your area. There are many Youtube videos and DVD's available. Signing up for a series of beginner lessons where you will have an instructor will help you coordinate the movements with your breathing. From that solid beginning you can venture out to find the yoga practice that best suits you. Many of the poses are really not difficult and serve to slowly and safely stretch your body to keep it all working properly.

Here are some fun poses for beginners below. You can learn these and honestly say to people "oh, I know a few yoga poses!"

The corpse pose: Lie on the floor with arms 45 degrees to body, full feet outward, close your eyes and relax. This is a good one to do when you are feeling stressed.

Just stop and rest your body. Put your timer on for 2 minutes and be still. If you fall asleep you probably needed more sleep. Any way you look at it, this is the pose that will relax you. Try it now. How do you feel? _____

Prayer pose is another easy one. Stand straight with your feet together and your arms to your side. Roll your shoulders back so you are nicely upright. Take a long deep breath and on the exhale bring your arms up with palms of your hands facing and touching each other and even with your nose. This helps you remember to stand tall and straight and breathe. It is so simple but you just feel better doing it. Try it now _____ How did you feel? _____

The Mountain pose, called Tadasana, is a basic pose, deceptively simple. It is just standing. Easy but you need to focus. It requires balancing. It helps you attain your inner balance. Hands are at the side dropping pointed to the earth. We are often used to standing against something or over to the side. This pose asks you to stand tall with weight evenly on both feet. Breathe. As you do this think "I am a mountain." "I am the stability of the mountain." Try it now. How do you feel? _____

And then there is Vrikshasana…**the tree pose.** You know of this one. Standing still, you raise both hands above your head, palm touching palm AND you lift one leg and slowly move it up to rest on the other thigh. Not so easy. But if you keep practicing you can get it. Try it now and note how far you can get that moving leg up against the other leg? Try it several times and you will be amazed how quickly you can do it when you are focusing. How do you feel? _____ The hands above you do help the balance.

Last one I will mention, is the **Sun Salutation.** This is a warm-up exercise of 12 movements calling you to stretch back and forward, stretch each leg out in back of you and fold down bending the waist. Parts of this pose are included in many others and is a good way to begin your practice or just to begin the day, if you are rushing off. It does not take long. This is too much to do now.

Now you can do 4 poses: Corpse, Prayer, Mountain and Tree. Do the corpse pose every time you feel stressed and give it at least 2 minutes on your phone timer.

I have one of the many available DVD's for yoga, made by Rodney Yee. He leads you in a 20 minute morning workout. I recommend it to you. I also encourage you to keep at your yoga practice if you have one and if not to try an in-person class, go online and/or purchase or download a DVD to work with at home or wherever you are.

Qigong/Tai Chi

Tai Chi: What is it?

"Tai Chi practice is both external and internal. The external aspect of Tai Chi teaches the martial arts applications, as well as exercise and health related routines. The internal aspect improves the circulation of the inner energy known as Qi (said chee) and it aids in the development of the performer's character."

This practice has three parts

1. The study and practice of formal routine known as **"forms"**. I would like to be able to do the Yang 40 form which includes 40 movements. Each of these movements makes its way into the next. If you learn it and are adept, it is looking like a dance. I picture myself doing this on the front patio as the sun rises in perfect weather!

2. Meanwhile, I am working on a 22 minute am introduction in front of my computer screen at least 3 times a week. It is the second part of Tai Chi a series of moving meditations done in standing position known as **Qi-gong.** This is often referred to as "energy exercises" and helps in healing.

Both are very connected to the movements of nature, animals, birds, water and the names of the movements are often taken from nature. David Doran-Ross quotes a physician named Hua

Tuo who wrote "People are like water. Water moves and flows freely, is clean and healthy. But water that is stagnant breeds pestilence."

These practices produce bodies in motion, like a choreographed dance. And that leads to the third part of the practice.

3. Tai Chi can also be an **interactive game** for two people known as "pushing hands".

"From the beginning, centuries ago, Tai Chi was "meant to present a philosophy that places harmony and balance as the most desirable goals in life. They are the keys to inner peace, as well as a safe and peaceful society. For more that 500 years, practitioners of Tai Chi have discovered generation after generation that living by these principles has led to health, longevity, success and inner peace." Dorian-Ross

If you are interested in Tai Chi/Qigong, I highly recommend you watch the DVD's by David Dorian Ross, especially *"Essentials of Tai Chi and Qigong"*. He is not just describing movements and telling history. He is a living example of the peace, serenity and positive attitude he teaches. You will want to study with him and learn and you can. He has other DVD's with Tai Chi practices as well as *"Mastering Tai Chi"* another Great Courses offering.

Both Yoga and Tai Chi/Qigong are taught world wide and most cities have many teachers, even centers where each practice is taught. They both teach much more than the movements. Look for instructors who are living the philosophies of these two wonderful practices. You experience something very deep and enriching when you practice with others. However each of these practices may easily be done alone in your home. Once you have the inexpensive equipment you need and a DVD to teach you, it becomes nearly as inexpensive as walking.

Tao Te Ching Chapter 28

Be a pattern for the world
If you are a pattern for the world,
The Tao will be strong inside you
and there will be nothing you can't do.

Know the personal
yet keep to the impersonal:
accept the world as it is.
If you accept the world as it is
the Tao will be luminous inside you
and you will return to your primal self

References

Sivananda Yoga Ventanta Centre, **Yoga 101 Essential tips** by Penquin, 1995

Joan Budilovsky & Eve Adamson, **The complete Idiot's Guide to Yoga** Alpha Books. 1998

Rodney Yee and Patricia Walden **A.M. and P.M. Yoga for beginners**

David Dorian-Ross, International Master Tai Chi Instructor **Essentials of Tai Chi and Qigong**. Published by The Great Courses. 24 lectures. **Mastering Tai Chi,** The Great Courses, 24 lectures. **T'AI CHI, beginning practice,** includes a 22 minute QiGong am workout, Taught by David Dorian-Ross and produced by Giam

Lao Tzu. **The Tao Te Ching** New English Version with forward and notes by Steven Mitchell, Harper Perennial 1988

WEEK 12

Lesson 59: What's Next?

Where are you now? and what's next?

Each week-end you were asked what habits you would like to change from that week's work, as well as which habits you actually committed to change. Now is time for a survey of where you are with your habit changes and what comes next.

Please consult your "Chronicle of Habit Changes" to review. At the end of each of the 12 weeks there has been a review of habits you want to change and those you are working on. Please refer to those sheets as you look at where you have been and where you are going in your work to change habits. Doing this will remind you of areas you intend to change and give you direction in completing the changes you want to make.

1. The changes you want to consider making

2. The changes you have committed to making

3. Your progress in making those changes

Remember not to think black and white. It is not a matter of you completely changing a habit or not at all. Life just does not usually flow that way.

If you are aware, most of the time, to walk away from dangerous grocery store aisles
or
pause and breathe before you say to your friend "you're not listening to me!!!!!"
or

If 4 out of 7 nights you get 7 hours sleep, even 2 nights or if it has been 0, at least you are aware. You can't turn back once you are aware. Progress is happening.

Little by little, you are beginning to walk your talk and next time it will be easier. It is a rare person that changes, sometimes life long habits, all of a sudden, never to return to unwanted behaviors.

You might also want to make up a list showing different areas (the ones listed below) in which you have changed habits or are working on changes, instead of just a list of habits by date. Doing this will highlight your greatest needs and the areas that you want to change. It will help you to be more specific when you do visioning about the integrated person you are creating. As you express your desires, they are already on their way to you. You seeing them and wanting them is what brings them to you.

The areas we have worked with during these months are:

Nutrition Fitness Sleep Emotions Mind Spirit

Stress Mindfulness Visioning Relationships

What have you consciously done to make an effort to change habits in each of these areas? Which habits? Doing this review will help you stay on track.

Try to come back as often as you can to work on the changes. Put a personal review session on your calendar once a month to do a check. I go on a yearly one week retreat to check up on myself. I am off alone, where I am totally honest about who I am becoming and what parts of me need to increase and what parts decrease. Reviewing is work for today's lesson but tomorrow you begin a real celebration of the changes and our time together.

Thank you for your self determination.
Both hands clapping

WEEK 12

Lesson 60: Celebrating

This is far from the end, but it is the end of our 12 weeks together. Thank you for walking this with me. You were there with me long before you read this and really before I wrote it. It was you who gave me the courage to lose my weight and seek an integrated whole and joyous life. I saw you inside of me, just like me, struggling to be loved, to love myself, struggling to be what I thought the world wanted so I'd be approved. Then learning that sometimes what the world wants to approve is not lovely and true and of good report and that's what I wanted me to be. So I struggled again to find my alignment with Source and with myself.

There is no time here for guilt, so we are not going back to hover over what we did not do. Yesterday you reviewed what you did do.

If you are much overweight, 3 months isn't enough to lose it all. But write here also the weight progress.

12 weeks ago I weighed _____. And today I weigh _____.

Some of the habits I am most proud to have changed are:

These are the ones I am making good progress in changing:

Have you been able to let go of parts of yourself which you now know have worked against your wholeness? Which parts?

What was most difficult of these 3 months?

What was easiest?

What did you discover about your own ability to make this change?

Who and what was support for you? Please thank your friends and family who have stood by you and helped you.

You have walked with me through 90 days, three months, reading daily and doing what you could, congratulations! Everything you read, and all the effort you made is recorded right there in your subconscious mind and if you need to be reminded, just talk to those cells and they will continue to support you and lead you aright.

You have everything right there in you to make all your dreams come true!

Make good dreams and good visions and the world will be a better place

We walk together into our new habits of living
that continue to transform our bodies, minds, emotions
and increase our deep spiritual selves to come forth.

Other people will clap for you at your positive healthy changes, now and as you continue becoming something else.You also may be disappointed when they do not notice you have lost 50 pounds since the last time they saw you. If you feel your body responding with disappointment, please remember that they are dealing with their own stuff and the only person who really needs to cheer you on every day is the person you see in the mirror every day. Have I told you lately that you are magnificent? You are magnificent! You are loved. Take both your hands (don't stop to think this is silly, just do it) hold them on top of each other and press in to your heart and breathe, smile, release. See that wasn't hard. You can even do that when you are walking quietly through the crowd.

Keep celebrating there is always something to celebrate. You are in the breath of my heart as you continue to awaken to your beauty, inner and outer.

May all beings be at peace, live in harmony and be kind.

Cynthia+

There is one thing we can count on,
it's that endings will always be followed by new beginnings.
May you begin anew to build and maintain your beautiful, healthy you.

POSTSCRIPT

The light of the world is wherever you are
Evolution happens within us by saying "yes"
To the dare to believe that we can.

When we imagine it and visualize it, we can create it.
Be about creating your integrated healthy life
Live well, live long and prosper!

APPENDIX

Menu form

Dairy Products

Fruit

Leafy Green Vegetables

Menus for week of _____ to _____

Day	Breakfast	Lunch	Dinner	snacks	water

MONDAY

TUESDAY

WEDNESDAY

THURSDAY

FRIDAY

SATURDAY

SUNDAY

NOTES

SOME DAIRY DEFINITIONS

Butter is made by churning fresh or fermented cream or milk. It is generally used as a spread and a condiment, as well as in cooking, such as baking, sauces, pan flying. Butter consists of butterfat, milk proteins and water.

Yogurt is a semi-solid sourish food produced by bacterial fermentation of milk. Soy milk, nut milks such as almond milk and coconut milk can also be used. Bacteria used to make yogurt are known as "yogurt cultures".

Buttermilk refers to a number of dairy drinks. Originally buttermilk was the liquid left behind after churning butter out of cream. This type of buttermilk is known as *traditional buttermilk.*

Condensed milk is milk from which water has been removed. It is most often found in the form of sweetened condensed milk with sugar added.

Cottage cheese is a cheese curd product with a mild flavor. It is drained, but not pressed so some whey remains and the individual curds remain loose.

Cream is composed of the higher butterfat layer skimmed from the top of milk before homogenization. In non homogenized milk, the fat, which is less dense, will eventually rise to the top.

Cream cheese A soft, mild tasing cheese with a high fat content. Traditionally, it is made from unskimmed milk enriched with additional cream. Stabilizers such as carob bean gum and carrageenan are added.

Evaporated milk Also known as dehydrated milk, evaporated milk is a shelf-stable canned product with about 60% of the water removed from fresh milk. It differs from sweetened condensed milk, which contains added sugar.

Goat milk Goats produce about 2% of the worlds total annual milk supply. Some goats are bred specifically for milk.

Ice cream A frozen dessert usually made from dairy products, such as milk and cream and often combined with fruits or other ingredients and flavors.

Kefir is a fermented milk drink prepared by inoculating cow, goat or sleep milk with kefir grains.

Milk is a white liquid produced by the mammary glands of mammals. It is the primary source of nutrition for young mammals before they are able to digest other types of food.

Powdered milk is a manufactured dairy product made by evaporating milk to dryness. One purpose of dying milk is to preserve it. Milk powder has a far longer shelf life than liquid milk and does not need to be refrigerated, due to its low moisture content.

Processed cheese is a food product made from normal cheese and sometimes other unfermented dairy ingredients, plus emulsifiers, extra salt, food colorings, or whey. Many flavors, colors and textures of processed cheese exit.

Sour cream is obtained by fermenting a regular cream with certain kinds of lactic acid bacteria. The bacterial culture, which is introduced either deliberately or naturally, sours and thickens the cream.

Whey is the liquid remaining after milk has been curdled and strained. It is a by-product of the manufacture of cheese or casein and has several commercial uses.

Whipped cream "heavy cream" is cream that has been beaten by a mixer, whisk or fork until it is light and fluffy. Whipped cream is often sweetened and sometimes flavored with vanilla, and is often called Chantilly cream or creme Chantilly.

Alternates for those who are lactose intolerant:

Soy milk made from soy not cow's milk

Coconut milk made from coconuts.

Almond milk contains neither cholesterol nor lactose, and is often consumed by those who are lactose-intolerant and others who wish to avoid dairy products, including vegans. Commercial almond milk comes in sweetened, unsweetened, plain, vanilla and chocolate flavors, and is usually fortified with micronutrients.

Content of dairy product information from
From. <u>Dairy Nutrition Facts - Midwest Dairy</u>
https://www.midwestdairy.com/nutrition-and-health/dairy-nutrition/

LIST OF FRUIT

Apples "an apple a day can keep the doctor away"
it appears is still a viable saying!

- Apples can help lower the risk of heart disease, prevent constipation, control diabetes and prevent cancer.
- the skin is best and contains about 4 mg of quercetin, an antioxidant compound.
- a 5 ounce apple w/skin has about 3 grams of fiber
- can relieve constipation, prevent diverticulosis, and cancer of the colon
- excellent weight control food to loose weight without being hungry all the time.
- Helps lower cholesterol and the pectin forms a gel that slows digestion, which slows the rise in blood sugar
- average size apple has more pectin than strawberries or bananas.
- one medium apple is 80 calories

"Don't count on apple juice. Although apple juice contains a little iron and potassium, it's no great shakes compared to the whole fruit. By the time the apples wind up in juice, they've given up most of their fiber and quercetin. Of course if you are choosing between soda and apple juice, by all means choose the juice. But don't use it as a substitute for the real thing." page 23 *"Food Remedies"*

There are 2,500 kinds of apples in the United States. There are Apple Festivals in many parts of the USA where apples are a dominant crop. Enjoy discovering the varieties and flavors of the Apple!

Apricots

- help protect the eyes and prevent heart disease
- they are high in a mineral needed to produce sex hormones

- contain compounds that can fight infections, blindness and heart disease
- have beta-carotene which is a health protecting property, 3 fruits = 2 milligrams about 30 percent of recommended daily amount. This converts to vitamin A in the body
- also 3 fruits = 3 grams of fiber, 12 percent of Daily requirement
- eat the skin, most fiber there
- eat them firm, as they soften the nutrient compounds begin to break down
- avoid green apricots they may never ripen
- store in refrigerator in a plastic bag. They will keep about a week
- three medium apricots = 60 calories

Banana

- one of nature's best sources of potassium (provides 11% of Daily Value(DV)
- decrease risk of stroke and heart attack
- lower high blood pressure
- relieve heartburn, they seem to act as a natural antacid
- prevent and heal ulcers and infections
- speed recovery from diarrhea
- one 4.4 ounce Banana 110 calories

They are a good sources of electrolytes which you loose when you become dehydrated.

Too ripe? Put in refrigerator. They blacken, but inside will stop ripening when cooler.

Too green? Put in brown paper bag at room temp.

Berries

- can prevent cataracts
- ward off cancer
- prevent constipation
- and reduce the risk of infection
- "they have a compound called ellagic acid which is believed to help prevent cellular changes that can lead to cancer." Strawberries and Blackberries have the most ellagic acid
- Berries are very high in Vitamin C

Strawberries 8 medium 5.5 oz = 45 calories
Blueberries 1/2 cup = 41 calories
Raspberries 1 cup = 50 calories
Blackberries 1/2 cup = 37 calories

Cantaloupe

- is a type of muskmelon and full of healing substances that can help control
- blood pressure, lower cholesterol
- keep blood rushing smoothly and protect against cancer
- It is rich in Vitamin C and beta-carotene, both antioxidant compounds
- a source of potassium
- Purchase the melon ripe...should be heavy and have a sweet musky smell. If it does not smell sweet, choose another
- it has 113 % of DV of Vitamin C in 1 cup.
- Eat it quickly as the vitamin C degrades quickly after being cut.

1/2 a 5" cantaloupe = 94 calories

Cherries

- 1 cup, 21 cherries = 90 calories
- can help relieve gout
- prevent a variety of cancers
- reduce risk of stroke and heart disease
- best May-July
- stems should be green, if dark they have been sitting too long
- they are very perishable. They only keep for a few days so buy what you can eat.
- refrigerate but do not wash until ready to eat.
- they have vitamin C, A and E
- they have quercetin, which help block damage by free radicals, that is unusable oxygen molecules in the body.
- can significantly reduce risk of stroke, cancer
- eat them raw as cooking destroys some of the Vitamin C and other nutrients.

Folklore has it that cherries drive away gout. In fact, Dr Steve Schumacher, a kinesiologist in Louisville,Kentucky recommends eating cherries daily for gout.This was recorded in Prevention Magazine. He recommends to quit eating red meat and organ meats and to drink 2 or 3 glasses of cherry juice a day (black cherry juice diluted with an equal amount of water). He says good results within 24 to 72 hours, some a week. This depends on the severity of gout.

Cranberries

- 1/2 cup cranberries = 23 calories
- can help prevent and treat urinary tract infections
- usually suggested to drink cranberry juice, 10 oz daily
- among women with infections, those who took daily cranberry drink where 75% more likely to clear up the inflection.
- Blueberry juice is similar
- raw is better than cooked
- try a relish: cranberries(12 oz pkg), apple(1 med),1 orange, a scant 1/2 cup of pure maple Syrup and ground ginger(1/8 teaspoon)
- protect cells from cancerous changes
- reduce the risk of heart disease and stroke
- they are so tart that people often add sugar, which is an obstacle to their usefulness especially for those of us loosing weight

Currants

- 1/4 cup = 130 calories
- protect agains cancer
- reduce cholesterol
- lower risk of heart disease
- prevent constipation
- 1/2 cup of currents has 160 % of Daily Value

"Fresh currents are scarce in the USA because early in the 1900's the US Department of Agriculture banned their cultivation because the shrubs harbored a fungus that destroyed white pines." Selene Yeager p. 170 The ban was lifted in 1960 but the comeback has never materialized. Black currents sold in the markets are really zante grapes. Currents have ellagic acid which may stop cancer before it develops. raspberries, strawberries and grapes also have ellagic acid.

Dr Stoner, director of the cancer chemo-prevention program at the Ohio State University Comprehensive Cancer Center in Columbus, Ohio, suggests that 4-6 servings of fruit with ellagic acid a day, would substantially lower your risk of developing cancer. Eating 1 or 2 servings a day along with extra fruits and vegetables "provides all the fiber you need to keep your circulation in the swim."

Figs

- 1 med fig 2 oz = 38 calories
- can lower high blood pressure
- relieve constipation
- control cholesterol
- Can help prevent colon cancer

Figs are a great source of fiber, with much potassium. They also add Vitamin B6.

Helps you eliminate waste more quickly. "Figs are particularly good for people who are overweight because they are so high in fiber, stay in the stomach longer, helping people eat less. And they are very sweet. So they satisfy this sweet cravings."

Grapefruit

1/2 medium grapefruit = 60 calories

They can relieve cold symptoms, prevent cancer, reduce bruising and prevent heart disease. It has a sour taste. The red variety is often considered best as it contains more "lycopene which is an antioxidant and free radical scan vender". An excellent source of Vitamin C.

"When you eat Grapefruit you are essentially getting a chemical "mop" that helps clean up problems as they occur. "In animal studies, James Gerda, M D, found that grapefruit could produce a drop in Cholesterol of 21 percent. At the same time it helped prevent sticky components in blood, called platelets from forming clots in the bloodstream and increasing the risk of heart disease and stroke."

Grapes

- 1.5 cups grapes = 90 calories
- Grape juice has potassium and flavonoids.

Both wine and grape juice contain powerful compounds that help lower cholesterol, prevent hardening of the arteries and fight heart disease. Flavonoids lower rates of heart disease, and are among the most powerful antioxidants. "In your body they help prevent low density lipoprotein(LDL) Cholesterol from oxidizing - the process that enables cholesterol to stick to your artery walls and create blockages."

You need 3 x the amount of grape juice to get the same beneficial effects as wine.

Lemons and Limes

- 1 medium lemon = 15 calories
- One 2" diameter lime = 20 calories

Both can help heal cuts and bruises, prevent cancer and heart disease. The pulp and juice contain rich sources of Vitamin C. A large lemon contains 75 % of Daily Value.

Vitamin C lowers levels of Histamine, a chemical that can cause red eye and runny nose. It is a powerful antioxidant helping prevent cancer and heart disease. It helps heal cuts and wounds

Oranges

- 1 5.4 oz orange = 70 calories.
- One orange contains 117% of Daily Value.

It has the sweet taste of citrus, lowers risk of heart and stroke, stops inflammation and fights cancer and aids healing and boosts immunity.

Oranges are rich in natural sugars for quick energy. They contain: limonite, limonene, limonin glucoside and hesperidia, all of which show promise for blocking cancer and. contain compounds that may be able to stop heart attacks before they start. Cooking and freezing navel oranges can turn them bitter. They are best at room temperature.

Pears

- 1 med 5.9 oz = 100 calories,
- 2 pears give you 32 % of Daily Value.

"They help lower cholesterol, improve memory and alertness and keep bones

strong. They contain lignin which helps remove cholesterol from the body and insoluble fiber. It acts like Velcro, trapping the cholesterol molecules in the intestine before they get absorbed int the blood stream. Because lignin cannot pass through the intestinal wall, it goes into the stool, taking cholesterol along with it."

Pears also have insoluble fiber that does not dissolve in the intestine. What it does however, is absorb large amounts of water. This causes stools to pass more easily and quickly through the digestive tract, which helps prevent constipation and hemorrhoids and also reduces the risk of colon cancer.

Pineapple

- 2 slices 3" diameter = 60 calories.

Helps keep bones strong, improves digestion, relieves cold symptoms and lowers the risk of cancer and heart disease. Rich in vitamin C, a cup of fresh pineapple chucks or drinking pineapple juice will give you 2 milligrams of manganese, more than 100 % Daily value."The body uses manganese to make collagen, a tough fibrous protein that helps build connective tissues like bone, skin and cartilage, preventing osteoporosis."

Plantains

- 1 3 oz plantain = 100 calories.

They are ulcer protection and help lower blood pressure

Prevent & treat ulcers, prevent constipation and decrease the risk of heart disease. You need to cook plantains, not eat them raw. They are a starchy fruit full of potassium, and magnesium. "Experts are not sure how they do it, but plantains are known for their ability to both prevent and treat ulcers as well as to quell digestive upset such as flatulence and indigestion."

Prunes

- 1/4 cup = 110 calories.

Nature's laxative. They can relieve constipation, lower cholesterol and reduce the risk of cancer & heart disease. One serving or about 5 prunes is enough to keep most people "regular". "They are high in insoluble fiber, have a natural sugar called sorbitol and contain a compound called dihydroxyphenyl which stimulates the intestine causing it to contract. This process is necessary for having regular bowel movements"

Raisins

- 1/4 cup = 130 calories.

Can help improve digestion, lower blood pressure and keep blood healthy. They are a high energy convenient snack that almost never go bad.

A good source of potassium, rich in iron, can be a better source than meat.

"Iron is essential for the creation of hemoglobin in red blood cells, which the body uses to transport oxygen. They are also a good source of dietary fiber

Rhubarb

Provides relief from constipation, can help lower cholesterol, prevent cancer, boost immunity and ease digestive problems and is rich in vitamin C and fiber.

Only eat the stalks. The leaves can be toxic. It is a member of the buckwheat family and is a good source of fiber. It can sop up cholesterol and flush it from your body before it gets a chance to stick to your arteries, clogging them up and contributing to heart disease.

The easiest way to cook it is to chop the stems into small pieces, add cinnamon and 3/4 cup of Maple syrup to 4 cups of fruit, and cook down slowly to a sauce. You can eat it by itself or over yogurt.

Tangerines

• 1 medium = 50 calories.

They are small Mandarin oranges that originated in China, where most citrus fruits originate. They are rich in vitamin C, and beta-cryptoxanthin, as well as the compounds tangeretin and nobiletin. These work against some types of breast cancer. Researchers in Japan are finding that tangeretin could inhibit the growth of leukemia cells.

Also present in tangerines is the compound called beta-cryptoxanthin, "which turns into Vitamin A in the body. 8 oz of tangerine juice can give you 20% of Vitamin A Daily value." Both A and C vitamins are antioxidants that can stop free radicals from damages leading to everything from wrinkles and heart disease to cancer. Tangerines are in season from October into May.

References for fruits

Goodman, Prof Anthony A, Montana State University, **Lifelong Health: Achieving Optimum Well-being at Any Age.** The Great Courses 2010.

Selene Yeager and Editors. **The Doctor's Book of Food Remedies.** 1998. Rodale Press

Leafy Greens

Kale is very popular now. I stayed away, not liking my first quick taste, until a friend served me a kale salad made with kale chopped small, then chopped again and again.

She added a sweet dressing and chopped onion with a few very small chopped red peppers. I was hooked. Now I mostly chop it but not all that small and put it in most of my salads. You don't have to have someone else's recipe, just go online and look up kale recipes! Kale is an excellent source of vitamins A, C and K, a lot of calcium as well as folate and potassium. Carotenoids and flavonoids are the specific types of antioxidants associated with many of its anti-cancer health benefits.

Kale is also rich in the eye-health promoting lutein and zeaxanthin compounds. Beyond antioxidants, the fiber content of cruciferous kale binds bile acids and helps lower blood cholesterol levels and reduce the risk of heart disease, especially when kale is cooked instead of raw. Kale's ruffled edges are cream, black or purple, depending upon the variety.

Nutritional info: One cup is 70 calories no fat 4 g of protein. 10 g carbs and 5 g of fiber.

Collard Greens

Are similar in nutrition to kale & cabbage and have become indispensable in the healthcare industry. But they have a heartier and chewier texture and a stronger cabbage-like taste. They are an unknown and under-appreciated vegetable for many people. They are also popular with the raw food movement because the wide leaves are used as a wrapper instead of tortillas or bread.

Nutritional Info: (One Cup) 25 calories, 0g fat, 2g protein, 5g carbs, 3g fiber

Benefits: Collard green leaves are laden with fiber which minimizes the severity of LDL "Bad" cholesterol in blood. Collard Greens can be eaten regularly to build up excellent resistance power in the body to control the onset of colon cancer, acute bowel disorder problems and hemorrhoid disorder. Collard leaves perform as an anti-oxidant to purify the body, and this detoxification is done well if an individual eats collard greens on regular basis.These vegetables contain vitamin K and other minerals, ensuring better bone development, formation of healthy cells and to some extent it reduces the severity of Alzheimers which damages the neural system. It also minimizes the destructive impact on human brain. At the same time, it increases the physical stamina and energy greatly.

Turnip Greens:

If you buy turnips with the tops on, you get two vegetables in one. Turnip leaves another Southern favorite are considered a delicacy. More tender than other greens and needing less cooking, this sharp-flavored leaf is low in calories yet loaded with vitamins A,C, and K as well as calcium. Turnip greens leafy, green tops, have grown in popularity across the rest of the United States thanks to their assertive flavor and hearty nutritional profile. When you're buying turnip greens, choose ones with consistent color, crisp leaves and slender stems.

Nutritional Info: (One Cup) 20 calories, 1 g fat 1.2 g of protein, 4.4 g of carbohydrates and 3.5 g fiber

Benefits: Turnip Greens are rich in Vit A which acts as an antioxidant and promotes healthy eyesight as well as preventing certain age-related eye disorders.They provide iron, and calcium. Eating vitamin A-rich foods help your body target and get rid of toxins and free radicals that can contribute to cancer. Iron is important because it is responsible for the formation and development of healthy red blood cells, which ensure that enough oxygen is circulated throughout your body. An iron deficiency can also lead to anemia, (low red blood cell count) and can cause fatigue, pale skin and breathlessness.

Turnip greens provide calcium which is good for your bones and teeth, and a diet high in calcium may prevent softening of the bones, bone fractures and osteoporosis. A 1-cup serving of turnip greens provides 32 mg of magnesium that helps your body absorb and use calcium. The same serving of turnip greens also contains 5 g of fiber and 1.6 g of protein. Turnip greens supply potassium, as well as the vitamin C and vitamin K. An adult needs 1000 mg of calcium each day, and a 1-cup serving of cooked turnip greens will add 197 mg.

Swiss Chard:

With red stems, stalks, and veins on its leaves, has a beet-like taste and soft texture that's perfect for sautéing. Both Swiss chard and spinach contain oxalates, which are slightly reduced by cooking and can bind to calcium, a concern for people prone to kidney stones. Chard is a good source of vitamins A and C.

Nutritional Info: (One Cup) 7 calories, 0.7 protein, 0.07 fat, 0.6 fiber and 1.4 g carbs.

Benefits: One cup of cooked leaves of Swiss Chard has enough calcium to support healthy bones and prevent osteoporosis. When added with vitamin K1, it plays a great role in preventing excessive action by the cells that break down bone. Swiss chard is full of antioxidants along with vitamin K; vitamin C and vitamin A. It helps to prevent and treat coronary artery disease and various other diseases. It helps to prevent inflammation, contains the daily recommended content of potassium, which helps to maintain the level of blood sugar, along with containing high amount of fiber content that helps to reduce blood cholesterol.

Swiss chard maintains proper heart health with its stores of vitamin K and helps to maintain clotting of normal blood. Presence of magnesium content helps to deal with various cardiovascular diseases, and as a helps to deal with hypertension. Swiss chard is good for skin maintenance and skin health, by boosting skin glow. Presence of vitamin A along with vitamin C plays a great role in the production of collagen, providing skin health and prevention of acne.

Vitamin A and vitamin C are essential to stimulate and improve the immune system. The vitamin A in Swiss chard also helps to protect your eyes against macular degeneration and is useful for people suffering for anaemia, because of its iron content. The leafy vegetable also houses B complex vitamins, which helps to cure tiredness and depression, while it prevents Alzheimer's, various types of cancer and controls diabetes.

Swiss chard looks great in your garden or in pots, is easy to grow and tastes even better when you cook or use it in salad, fresh picked!

Spinach:

One of the most nutrient-dense foods in existence, spinach is low in calories and packed with vitamins A and C, as well as folate. Cooked spinach gives you more nutrition than raw, but is excellent eaten raw in salads.

Nutritional Info: (One Cup) 7 calories, 0.12g Fat, 0.86g Protein, 1.09g Carbs., 4.3 Fiber

Benefits: Contains more than a dozen individual flavonoid compounds, which work together as cancer-fighting antioxidants. Spinach reduces cholesterol and its magnesium works toward healthy blood pressure levels. It contains a carotenoid that makes prostate cancers destroy themselves. This same carotenoid, after being changed by the intestines, prevents prostate cancer from reproducing itself. Spinach also contains kaempferol, a strong antioxidant that prevents the formation of cancerous cells. Women who have a high intake of this flavonoid show a reduced risk of ovarian cancer. Spinach protects your brain function from premature aging and slows old age related effects on your mental capabilities. This is accomplished by preventing the harmful effects of oxidation on your brain. Those who eat vegetables in quantity, especially those of the leafy green variety, experience a decrease in brain function loss. Are you listening?

Mustard Greens:

Similar nutrition profile to turnip greens and collards, mustard greens have scalloped edges and come in red and green varieties. They have a peppery taste and give off a mustardy smell during cooking. Their spiciness can be toned down by adding an acid, such as vinegar or lemon juice, toward the end of cooking.

Nutritional Info: (One Cup) 15 Calories, 0.1 g Fat, 1.5g Protein, 2.7 g Carbs., 1.8g Fiber

Benefits: Mustard greens help reduce the risk of certain types of cancers such as bladder, breast, colon, lung, prostate, and ovarian cancer. They promote heart health by lowering cholesterol. Folate in mustard greens also plays an important part in keeping the heart healthy. They even contain a small amount of glucoraphanin which provides important anti-inflammatory benefits and reduces unwanted inflammation.

Mustard greens are great source of Vitamin A. High in Vitamin C and magnesium, these are good to cure asthma as they help lungs to stay relaxed and avoid any constriction. Magnesium also helps to regulate and control blood pressure levels. They are also good in the prevention of certain menopausal symptoms.

Broccoli: is a veritable goldmine of nutrition, rich in vitamins C and A, potassium, and folate. It's stalks and florets add both crunch and color to stir-fries.

Nutritional Info: (One Cup) 30 Calories, 0g Fat, 2g Protein, 6g Carbs., 2g Fiber

Benefits: Broccoli's potassium, helps maintain a healthy nervous system and optimal brain function, as well as promotes regular muscle growth. Its magnesium and calcium help regulate blood pressure. Broccoli also has high levels of calcium and vitamin K, both important for bone health and prevention of osteoporosis.

Broccoli helps repair skin damage and allows skin detoxification and repair. Its vitamin C serves as an effective antihistamine to ease the discomfort of the common cold. Also, one cup of broccoli bolsters the immune system with a large dose of beta-carotene also providing trace minerals, zinc and selenium. Broccoli is a good source of vitamin A that is needed to form retinal, the light-absorbing molecule that is essential for both low-light and color vision. As a diet aid Broccoli is high in fiber, which promotes digestion, prevents constipation, maintains low blood sugar, and curbs overeating.

Rapini (Broccoli Rabe):

Rapini looks a lot like broccoli but is actually a member of the turnip family. It is a big part of many Chinese and Italian dishes, an easy addition to many stir fry and pasta dishes.

Nutrition Info: (One Cup) 9 Calories, 0g fat, 1g protein, 1g carbs, 1g fiber

Benefits: This is a cancer-preventing powerhouse full of phytochemicals. Like all Brassicas, it's a rich source of glucosinolates, which your body converts to cancer-fighting sulforophanes and indoles.

A 3 1/2-ounce serving of broccoli rabe provides more than half your daily requirement of antioxidant-rich vitamins A and C, both of which fight off dangerous free radicals that can cause damage to your body's cells, is also a good source of folate (a B vitamin that protects against birth defects and heart disease), not to mention potassium, fiber, and calcium and vitamin K. Rapini contains strong anti-inflammatory nutrients, such as folate and vitamin C. Both nutrients reduce homocysteine, a type of amino acid that can damage the arteries causing coronary heart disease. It has 2 grams of fiber/cup, helps detoxify the liver, it maintains a healthy hormonal balance for both men and women and will reduce yeast infections in the body, because it kills Candida albicans, the yeast strain that often overgrows when we take anti-biotics.

Bok Choy:

Bok Choy, (or Baby Bok Choy) or Chinese cabbage, like Rapini and Spinach is packed with both vitamin A and C. It can be wonderful and easy addition to any stir fry dish. If you want to experiment with it, try sautéing or stir-frying bok choy with chopped garlic and shredded ginger, or sesame oil and soy sauce. I usually steam it, then add a bit of butter and salt and pepper.

Nutrition Info: (One Cup) 9 calories, less than 1g fat, 1g protein, 2 g carbs, 1 g fiber

Benefits: Bok Choy is a low-calorie low fat, low carb vegetable, perfect to add to many dishes, plus Bok choy is rich in antioxidant content, especially beta carotene, which contributes in warding off various diseases such as cancer. Carotenoids are also thought to benefit eye health, and help reduce the chances of macular degeneration. It also offers lots of vitamin A, vitamin C and vitamin K. In fact, one cup of shredded raw bok choy contains about half of your daily requirement for each of these nutrients. Plus, you'll get healthy levels of folate and vitamin B6, as well.

Bok Choy is listed as one of the "150 Healthiest Foods on Earth," and a particularly good vegetable for controlling your weight and losing pounds. It is one of the healthiest low-calorie foods you can eat.

Red and Green Leaf and Romaine Lettuce

These lettuces are high in vitamin A and offer some folate. Leaf lettuces have a softer texture than romaine, a crunchy variety used in Caesar salads. Fans of Iceberg lettuce may go for romaine, a crispy green that's better for you. The darker the lettuce leaf, the more nutrition it has, making red leaf slightly healthier than green.

Nutrition Info: (One Cup) 4 calories, 0.06 g fat, 0.37 g protein, 0.63 g of carbohydrates and 0.3 g fiber.

Benefits: Red Leaf lettuce is packed with vitamins, minerals and amino acids.

Red Leaf Romaine contains minerals essential for your body to make bones, produce hormones and regulate your heartbeat. Deficiencies in minerals can cause health complications like osteoporosis from lack of calcium. That one-cup serving of red leaf lettuce contains 9 milligrams of calcium, it also contains iron, magnesium, phosphorus, potassium, sodium, zinc, copper, manganese and selenium.

Cabbage:

Although paler in color than other leafy greens, this cruciferous vegetable is a great source of cancer-fighting compounds and vitamin C. It is considered the workhorse of the kitchen. Available in red and green varieties, cabbage can be cooked, added raw to salads, tacos or stir fries, shredded into a slaw, or made into sauerkraut.

Nutrition Info: (One Cup) 22 calories, 0g fat, 1g protein, 5g carbs, 2g fiber.

Benefits: Cabbage ranks right up there with broccoli, cauliflower, and Brussels sprouts with a reputation for fighting cancer. It's also a good source of vitamin C, fiber, potassium, and other nutrients. Cabbage also offers a major payoff, which is providing the fewest calories and least fat than any vegetable.

From green cabbage you'll enjoy a fiber boost and a respectable amount of vitamin C. Two other types of cabbage, savoy and bok choy also provide beta-carotene, the antioxidant that battles cancer and heart disease. For those who don't eat dairy products, these cabbages can be an important source of calcium, which helps prevent osteoporosis and aid in controlling blood pressure.

The phytochemicals in cabbage, called indoles, are also being studied for their ability to convert estradiol, an estrogen-like hormone that may play a role in the development of breast cancer, into a safer form of estrogen powerful incentives to add cabbage to your diet.

Cabbage can help you lose weight because it can be eaten in high volumes without providing higher calories. Foods higher in fiber like cabbage are very cleansing and will fill you up faster, resulting in less overall calorie consumption.

Watercress:

Watercress is a member of the cabbage family along with other greens such as mustard greens, kale, and turnip greens. Watercress offers similar health benefits as kale and collards and can be used in the same way. Slightly peppery and sour tasting watercress is handy because it can be added raw to salads or sandwiches without a minute of preparation time. Like the other veggies on this list, one cup has more than your daily value of vitamin K, and is also linked to cancer prevention.

Nutrition Info: (One Cup) 4 calories, 0g fat, 1g protein, 0g carbs, 0g fiber

Benefits: Watercress contains many phytochemicals, which are plant compounds that offer disease prevention. Watercress has a higher antioxidant concentration than apples or broccoli. Studies have found that baby leaf watercress contains more antioxidants than other greens.

Studies have also found that the antioxidants and carotenoids in watercress can reduce cellular damage related to the development of cancer. Researchers fed 30 smokers and 30 nonsmokers 85 g of raw watercress daily for 8 weeks. While all participants experienced benefits, the smokers benefits were far more significant. Watercress aids weight loss by adding bulk to meals without adding a lot of calories, helping you to feel full but not exceed your calorie limits. Watercress is also used to improve digestion, and *The Centers for Disease Control and Prevention recommend including more watercress in your diet to promote weight loss.* It also increases the amount of urine produced by the body, acting as a natural diuretic.

References

The Doctor's Book of Food Remedies by Selene Yeager

Prevention Health Books Rodale Press 1998

Online: thescienceofeating.com

Printed in the United States
By Bookmasters